CITIZEN AKOY

CITIZEN AKOY

Basketball and the Making of a South Sudanese American

Steve Marantz

University of Nebraska Press | Lincoln and London

Library of Congress Cataloging-in-Publication Data
Names: Marantz, Steve.
Title: Citizen Akoy: basketball and the making of a
South Sudanese American / Steve Marantz.
Description: Lincoln: University of Nebraska Press,
2019. | Includes bibliographical references and index.
Identifiers: LCCN 2018016699
ISBN 9781496203229 (hardback)
ISBN 9781496212580 (epub)
ISBN 9781496212597 (mobi)
ISBN 9781496212603 (pdf)
Subjects: LCSH: Agau, Akoy, 1994– | Basketball
players—United States—Biography. | Omaha Central
High School (Omaha, Neb.)—Basketball—History.
| Sudanese Americans—Biography. | Refugees—
South Sudan—Biography. | BISAC: SPORTS &
RECREATION / Basketball. | SOCIAL SCIENCE /
Ethnic Studies / African American Studies. | SOCIAL
SCIENCE / Emigration & Immigration.
Classification: LCC GV885 .M288 2019 | DDC
796.323092 [B]—dc23 LC record available at
https://lccn.loc.gov/2018016699

Set in Minion Pro by E. Cuddy.
Designed by L. Auten.

To Alison, my muse and light

No one wants to become a refugee. No one should have to endure this humiliating and arduous ordeal. Yet, millions do. Even one refugee forced to flee, one refugee forced to return to danger is one too many.

—Ban Ki-moon, UN Secretary-General

Contents

Acknowledgments

This story owes, first of all, to Akoy Agau, who was the primary source of information and whose cooperation was beyond generous. Just as instrumental was Akoy's mother, Adaw Makier, who reconstructed her refugee journey with pride and sadness. Akoy's father, Madut Agau, and Akoy's siblings were politely supportive of the process. I am thankful for their help and deeply respectful of their struggles and accomplishments.

My thanks to Akoy's confidantes: Scott, Leisha, and Trae Hammer; Dave, Ann, and Charlotte "Lotte" Sjulin; and Tarir "Ty" Gatuoch. Thanks also to Akoy's former Omaha Central High coaches and teammates: Jay Ball, Eric Behrens, Paulino Gomez, Tra-Deon Hollins, Jay Landstrom, Dominique McKinzie, K. J. Scott, Tre'Shawn Thurman, and Edward Vinson. Former Central coaches Rick Behrens, Chad Burns, and Herb Welling contributed, as did opposing coaches Bruce Chubick and Tim Cannon. Jay Landstrom's video highlight reels were an archival source.

More thanks to current and former Central High administrators and teachers Bette Ball, Edward Bennett, Keith Bigsby, Linda Ganzel, Gaylord "Doc" Moller, Rod Mullen, Paul Nielson, Denise Powers, Tim Shipman, Jen Stastny, and Michelle Synowiecki, as well as former Central students Emily Beck, Jacob Bigelow, Changkuoth Gatkuoth (formerly Lol Kuek), Henry Hawbaker, and Jen Rooney.

Central High Foundation executive director Michele Roberts offered her memories and resources, with the able assistance of communications manager Josh Bucy. Alumni historian Jim Wigton provided archival material on the struggle to save Central in the 1970s.

South Sudanese and African perspectives came from Omaha Talons founder Koang Doluony, Bernadita and Nancy Peter, Gutluak Kang of the

Refugee Empowerment Center, and attorney Amadu Swaray. Institutional viewpoints came from Susan Mayberger of Omaha Public Schools and Ryan Overfield and Lacey Studnicka of Lutheran Family Services of Nebraska. Mabel Boyd and Raydelle Meehan offered a history of the Mason School. Central alum A'Jamal Byndon offered an African American perspective.

Interviewees from media included Mike Sautter, who founded the website Nebraska High School Hoops, and Thor Tripp of KETV 7. Ryan Spring and Joe Mantegna at Blair Academy and Stu Vetter at Montrose Christian Academy were interviewed. Doug Goltz at Falls City Sacred Heart provided hoops history at his school.

Media sources included the *Albany Times-Union*, Alternet.org, *Anderson Independent-Mail*, *Breitbart News*, espn.com, *Grand Island Independent*, *Huffington Post*, *Idaho Statesman*, *Lincoln Journal Star*, *Louisville Courier Journal*, MaxPreps.com, *New Sudan Vision*, *New York Times*, *Omaha World-Herald*, Rivals.com, and *Washington Post*. Additional sources were the *Central High Register* and *Central High O-Books* from the late 1990s through 2013 and Leo Adam Biga's blog, *My Inside Stories*.

Books included *The Dinka of Sudan*, by Francis Mading Deng (Long Grove IL: Waveland Press, 1984); *The Middle of Everywhere*, by Mary Pipher (Orlando: Harcourt, 2002); *I Am a Man*, by Joe Starita (New York: St. Martin's Press, 2008); *What Is the What*, by Dave Eggers (New York: Vintage Books, 2007); *Play Their Hearts Out*, by George Dohrmann (New York: Ballantine Books, 2012); *Manute*, by Leigh Montville (New York: Simon and Schuster, 1993); *LeBron James: The Rise of a Star*, by David Lee Morgan Jr. (Cleveland: Gray and Company, 2003); *Brando: Songs My Mother Taught Me*, by Robert Lindsey (New York: Random House, 1994); *Brando's Smile*, by Susan Mizruchi (New York: Norton, 2014); *Bridge of Words: Esperanto and the Dream of a Universal Language*, by Esther Schor (New York: Metropolitan Books, 2016); *Notes from My Travels*, by Angelina Jolie (New York: Pocket Books, 2003); *Running for My Life*, by Lopez Lomong (Nashville: Thomas Nelson, 2012); *Of Beetles and Angels*, by Mawi Asgedom (New York: Little, Brown, 2001); and *Breaking Cardinal Rules*, by Katina Powell (Indianapolis: IBJ Book Publishing, 2015).

Karina Longworth's podcast "You Must Remember This" educated me on the Hollywood blacklist. Refugee data, reports, and analyses came from the office of the UN High Commissioner for Refugees; the Congressional Research Service; the Office of Refugee Resettlement; the Departments of State, Homeland Security, and Health and Human Services, and the Migration Policy Institute. Bronwen Manby provided a study on nationality rights in Sudan and South Sudan and a follow-up assessment.

Special thanks to Central High history teacher Scott Wilson for connecting pertinent faculty to me, critiquing my first draft, and inspiring students lucky enough to get a seat in his classroom.

My son, Alex Marantz, read the first draft and helped me shape the content. My wife, Alison Arnett, daughter Nora Marantz, son-in-law Luke Gaudreau, and daughter-in-law Rose Heydt provided moral support. The arrival of grandson Harris Gaudreau was a reminder that birth—be it a baby or a story—is both an agonizing and a blessed event.

Introduction

REFUGEE

History and hate chased Akoy Agau from his native Sudan as a little boy. He came to America as a refugee, and among what he learned was basketball. At Omaha Central High School, in love with the game, Akoy chased history and a place to belong. He came of age at the dawn of social media and with it posted a saga of hoops, hope, and salvation.

Nebraska and grassroots basketball gave him his audience, though the audience might well have included refugees and displaced persons worldwide had they been privileged to watch one of their own. As a six-year-old in Cairo, Egypt, Akoy was among an estimated twenty million refugees outcast from or displaced within their native lands on the occasion of the first World Refugee Day, June 20, 2001. Inaugurated by the UN High Commissioner of Refugees (UNHCR), its purpose was to recognize those who, as defined by law, were unable or unwilling to return to their home countries because of a "well-founded fear of persecution" due to race, political opinion, religion, nationality, or membership in a particular social group.

"Refugees are the great survivors of our time," said UN secretary-general Kofi Annan. "Many overcome immense hardship during years of exile, finally returning to their devastated countries to rebuild shattered communities. Others can never go home, and must forge new lives in strange lands. All of them deserve our encouragement, support and respect."

Annan spoke on the fiftieth anniversary of the 1951 UN Refugee Convention, which created a legal framework for refugee rights. That same day U.S. secretary of state Colin Powell honored several south Sudanese refugees at his Washington DC office. Powell's guests were "Lost Boys," so called because many had been conscripted against their will, orphaned, and subjected to peril and hardship. "They are representative of millions of people around the world who have been separated from their homes, separated from their loved ones and may never see their loved ones again, or people who are displaced within their countries," Powell said. "It is a worldwide tragedy that we have this consequence of war and other tragedies that cause people to be so displaced."

On the second World Refugee Day, in June 2002, seven-year-old Akoy was in Maryland as Powell honored refugee women in the nation's capital. "To look into the face of a refugee woman is to peer into the very eyes of the exodus," he said. "Mirrored in them are memories of fear and flight, of devastation and despair. But when those extraordinary eyes look back at you, they are also the eyes of hope, and surely they are the eyes of a heroine." Of the twenty-two million refugees counted by UNHCR, Powell said, eighteen million were women and children:

> We have seen it again and again, from Cambodia to Colombia, from Kosovo to Congo, from Liberia to Bosnia, from Sierra Leone to East Timor to Afghanistan. Wherever tyranny and terror, conflict and chaos, force families to flee their homelands, it is the women—it is the women—who become the most vulnerable to the worst kind of violence. And is it also the women who play the most vital roles in their families' survival.
>
> For them, every new day brings life or death, burdens and dangers. Most often it falls to refugee women to provide the family's income and to provide an education for the children. It is most often up to them to search for fuel, food, water, and medicine—the very bare essentials of life. They risk bullets, land mines and rape to provide the little that their families need just to survive.

Akoy was new to English, so he might not have grasped Powell's comments had he heard them. Then again, he did not need the U.S. secretary of state to tell him about his mother. She had escaped Sudan with him and his brother while his father was jailed. She had found a place to live in Cairo and had worked menial jobs to buy subsistence rations so they could eat. She had helped his father get to Cairo and had given birth to two more children. She had gotten him to America. Life would hurtle Akoy forward, and no matter where and how it sent him, he always would be his mother's son, in her debt.

As a teen, Akoy courted attention with the dignity and discipline of his role model, LeBron James, and with the artifice and cool of his alter ego, Ferris Bueller. He was so bold—or brazen—as to prophesize four state championships. He became the sum of his family, faith, and education and of his appetite for basketball, social media, and drama. Indeed he tweeted two days before his seventeenth birthday in 2011, "I need to be an actor!"

By then the global population of refugees and displaced persons had reached 44 million, on its way to 68.5 million in 2017. Nations and entire regions shuddered and convulsed while Akoy grew tall and strong. His parents found him a place to live—Nebraska!—and then he found a place to belong, on Facebook and Twitter, above the rim, and in the record book.

CITIZEN AKOY

Adaw

1

Akoy Agau was among nearly two million south Sudanese who fled their country from 1983 through 2004. His mother, Adaw Bak Madut Makier, was his guide and protector.

Adaw was born in 1974 outside the town of Wau, on the river Jur, in what was then the south of Sudan. She grew up on a farm and was "in the middle" of thirteen children who spoke Dinka, their tribal language, and Arabic. Ebony, tall, and slender, the Dinka were the largest tribe in south Sudan, known for "initiation" rites that scarred the foreheads and removed six lower teeth of their young men and for their devotion to cattle, of which they were said to be "loving slaves." Central to their culture were the concepts of *cieng* and *dheeng*, or unity and dignity.

The Dinka were one of the tribes in south Sudan who practiced Christianity and traditional beliefs and were long oppressed by Arab Muslims to the north. Arab Muslims had carried out slave raids on the southern tribes before Britain colonized Sudan in the late nineteenth century. In the twentieth century under British rule, light-skinned Arab Muslims segregated themselves from dark-skinned Christian and animist tribes, sowing division and conflict. The Republic of the Sudan, about one-fourth the geographic size of the United States, with nineteen major ethnic groups and about six hundred ethnic subgroups speaking more than one hundred languages and dialects, shed British control in 1956. The British transferred power to Arab Muslims, who in turn imposed Arab customs and beliefs on the population of 10.5 million. A toxic stew of racism, ethnic feuds, religious fundamentalism, and anarchy erupted into what is known as the First Civil War.

A truce declared in 1972 coincided with Adaw's early years. In the south it was a welcome period of peace and autonomy from Arabism. "We used to live by my [maternal] grandma because my grandma loved my father—they worked together and tended cows together; he was like her real son," Adaw recalled. "We stayed in my grandma's house and my mom's house. They were thatched and round with cone roofs. My dad grew the seed for both houses; he grew the corn because he was the only man in both houses. . . . We made our own peanut butter and fished with our dad. We gathered wood to cook our fish and ate it right there at the river. We didn't need to eat at home."

Cattle were integral to the social and spiritual values of the Dinka and provided many of their needs, starting with milk, which they considered the best and most noble of foods. Dried dung was used as fuel and fertilizer; urine as disinfectant; hides as bedding skins; and horns as snuffboxes, trumpets, and spoons. As a condition of marriage, a Dinka groom was expected to present cattle as gifts, or "bridewealth," to the bride's family.

"My dad had a lot of cows," Adaw recalled. "Also sheep and goats and a lot of chickens. If we needed some eggs, we got it from our farm. We got our own milk. I drank a lot of milk. At night he herded the cows back to the barn."

Adaw remembered her youth as uncomplicated and nurturing: "We didn't go to school. There was a school in the city very far away. A couple of cars went from the city to the village, but people just walked mostly. When you go to the city, you don't worry about putting your kids in school. You go to buy things, like a skirt. Back then they don't care so much about clothes—you could walk naked. You buy what you needed and walked back to the village. . . . There was a big love around us from my grandma and my dad and mom. Life was good."

In 1978–79 the Islamic Revolution swept through Iran. Shock waves hit Sudan, where leaders in the north, covetous of new oil fields in the south, declared all of Sudan an Islamic state and instituted Sharia law in 1983. In what is known as the Second Civil War, Adaw's father went off to fight for the southern rebels—the Sudanese People's Liberation Movement/

Army (SPLM/A). Adaw was a frightened girl when militia from the north attacked her village. "We saw the soldiers with the guns and the big things they drive, the tanks," Adaw said. "There was a lot of death. You don't know what to do. You just cry and cry."

She continued: "My grandmother said to my mom, 'Atong, you need to leave with your children.' And then her daughter, my auntie, who was pregnant with twins, got shot and killed when we tried to leave. My grandmother said, 'Atong, just leave—run!'

"We ran to the jungle. A lot of people were running and screaming. What do you do? The person next to you is shot and falls down. You need to save your life, and you are crying. You just run. You carry nothing; you leave everything.

"We went through a jungle to avoid both armies. We were running, hiding, running, hiding. It was very hot. No food, no drink, nothing. At night we slept under big plants with spreading leaves—we were afraid of wild animals. We found puddles of dirty water; people fought to drink from them. We drank the dirty water and got sick.

"We walked for seven days, a long way. Then we got to a place with a car."

Adaw rode with her family to Khartoum, the capital of Sudan, about 570 miles northeast of her village, and found sanctuary in a UN refugee camp. "We were happy to get there—we were going to be saved," Adaw said. "The UN was there to give us a place to live and some food and clothes. We didn't care about shoes—we just needed to live. But my brother and sister were sick from the dirty water. They died in the camp. He was five and she was three. Adaw recalls, "We were in the camp for a year and a half or two years. We had some stuff in the camp but not a lot of other stuff. My mom sold some of our food to get shoes and dresses for my sister and me. One day we asked about our dad. She told us he was killed in the war. . . . We were in the camp until my mom's uncle found us. He lived in Khartoum and had looked for us. He took us to his house."

Emanuel Bol, her great uncle, brought Adaw, her sister, and her mother into his home in Omdurman, a suburb of Khartoum. He also sheltered children who were unrelated but had been orphaned by the war. He fed and

3

clothed them on his small income from a job with the city or military—
Adaw wasn't sure which; the job shielded him from the systemic persecution of non-Muslims.

Adaw came of age in a culture in which Sharia law proscribed civil
liberties for women. All women, including non-Muslims, were required
to wear veils. They had virtually no legal right to land ownership and had
to defer to their husbands or male guardians in the management of assets.
All forms of credit were reserved for men. Polygamy was legal for men.
Women retained the right to divorce, but the custody of children aged six
or older reverted to men. Men beat their wives at home or in public without
penalty or punishment. Female circumcision, also known as female genital
mutilation, was commonly practiced on young girls.

A military coup in 1989 brought to power Lt. Gen. Omar Hassan Al-
Bashir, an authoritarian who squashed democratic efforts and dialed up
persecution of non-Muslims. St. Joseph's Catholic Church was the sanctuary preferred by Emanuel Bol.

"Every Sunday he loved to go to church," Adaw said. "On Saturdays he
told us, 'Tomorrow we go to God's house; everybody have to get ready.'
We didn't have a lot of clothes—maybe one dress and one skirt. The skirt
you wear at home and the dress you keep for Sunday. At night we have
to pray 'Hail Mary' in our language; he would tell us it's time to pray, and
then you have to go to sleep." Adaw added, "Church was someplace to go.
There wasn't a lot to do. The girls didn't go outside a lot; a lot of bad things
were going on. Girls didn't go to school because eventually they are going
to marry and have children. That was why we focused on religion. I loved
the church a lot."

Her uncle encouraged her to focus on family: "My uncle would tell us,
'You guys are rich.' We said, 'How come we are rich when we are sleeping
hungry and we don't have enough food in our tummy?' He would tell us
that you are rich when you have people. He said, 'I feel rich when I have
you guys around to take care of. I had no one to take care of, but after you
came, I feel rich.'"

Adaw grew into womanhood in Omdurman. When she was nineteen, her uncle arranged her marriage to Madut Agau, who was from Gogrial, about fifty miles from her hometown of Wau. Ten years her senior, Madut made his living as a peddler in Khartoum. His first wife and his father had died in the war, and his only son was missing and presumed dead. Of Madut's four brothers and three sisters only one brother had survived the war. Soft spoken and polite, Madut had been spared the tribal customs of facial scarification and dental extraction as a young man. "My uncle knew Madut," said Adaw. "He came from the village to the city and was a salesman of clothes and shoes. He was separated from his brother; his mom was the only one left. My uncle saw that Madut had a lot of things to survive with. He saw that I had grown into an adult, so he said, 'Why can't we put them together? They can help take care of each other.' . . . "That's how we met. We got married right away. We lived in my uncle's house."

Adaw and Madut married in 1993, the same year the Clinton administration placed Sudan on its list of states that sponsor terrorism and imposed upon it trade and economic sanctions. Islamic terrorist Osama Bin Laden had moved from Saudi Arabia to Khartoum in 1991, three years after he founded Al-Qaeda, and lived there until the Sudanese government expelled him in 1996 under pressure from the United States. In 1998 Bin Laden issued a fatwa to all Muslims: "The ruling to kill Americans and their allies—civilian and military—is an individual duty for every Muslim who can do it in any country in which it is possible to do it." In 2001 Bin Laden was in Afghanistan when he orchestrated the 9/11 attacks against Americans.

Akoy was born in November 1994 and was named for Madut's grandfather. Even as the civil war escalated and survival became more tenuous for non-Muslims in the capital city, two-year-old Akoy was baptized as Daniel Akoy Madut Maguy Akoy Agau at St. Joseph's. The United States closed its embassy in Khartoum in February 1996 and moved personnel to Nairobi, Kenya, due to security concerns. By the time their second son, Maguy, was born in 1997, Adaw and Madut kept to the shadows and lived in fear.

The U.S. State Department's Bureau of Democracy, Human Rights, and Labor detailed the peril of Sudanese non-Muslims in a 1999 report:

Government forces were responsible for extrajudicial killings and disappearances. Government security forces regularly tortured, beat, harassed, arbitrarily arrested and detained, and detained incommunicado opponents or suspected opponents of the Government with impunity. Security forces beat refugees, raped women, and reportedly harassed and detained persons on the basis of their religion. Prison conditions are harsh, prolonged detention is a problem, and the judiciary is largely subservient to the Government. The authorities do not ensure due process and the military forces summarily tried and punished citizens. The Government infringed on citizens' privacy rights. . . .

Authorities continued to restrict the activities of Christians, followers of traditional indigenous beliefs, and other non-Muslims, and there continued to be reports of harassment and arrest for religious beliefs and activities. Catholic priests report that they routinely are stopped and interrogated by police. Security forces also detained persons because of their religious beliefs and activities. . . .

Muslims may proselytize freely in the north, but non-Muslims are forbidden to proselytize. Foreign missionaries and religiously oriented organizations continue to be harassed by authorities, and their requests for work permits and residence visas are delayed. . . .

A Muslim man may marry a non-Muslim, but a Muslim woman cannot marry a non-Muslim, unless he converts to Islam. . . . Non-Muslims may adopt only non-Muslim children; no such restrictions apply to Muslim parents.

As Adaw recalled, "War got worse in the city. People just got killed—just like that. Young men and young women got killed—for no reason. We know there was a war in the villages, and we think we are okay in the city, but now that is not so."

At that point, Adaw's uncle advised them to flee:, "My uncle said to us, 'Okay, you guys need to leave because this city is going to be bad soon. I don't want to hear that somebody just got killed. You just need to leave.' It was devastating to hear, but he was right. We said, 'Where do we go?' And he said, 'You need to go to Egypt.' The people in the villages went south to Kenya and Ethiopia. But to go there from the city we would pass through the soldiers and much danger. It was safer to go north to Egypt."

Early in 1999 Adaw was pregnant with her third child. Madut was arrested, ostensibly for selling his wares on the street without a proper license, but in fact for being Christian in Khartoum. There would not be enough money to buy Madut's freedom if Adaw and her children and mother had to be fed, so Emanuel arranged passports for them as "tourists" to Egypt, Adaw recalled, "because if you tell them you are evacuating, they won't let you go." They packed sparse belongings and set out for Cairo, first by train and then by boat.

In Cairo, a metropolis of seventeen million, south Sudanese refugees numbered between thirty and forty thousand. Adaw and her two children moved in with an aunt who had a small apartment and children of her own. To feed themselves and their children Adaw and her aunt cleaned the homes of Egyptian families. "We left the children in the apartment by themselves—there was no school for them," Adaw said. "You clean all day, and some people pay you twenty Egyptian dollars. But if that person decided not to give you money, there was nothing you could do. If you refuse to leave, you be dead. Egyptian police never take your side, only the Egyptian side. . . . At night when I go home, I bought onion and some oil and red lentils to make a soup. I bought a grain that was like millet. We didn't eat meat—it cost too much."

Life in Egypt was "very difficult" because refugees had no rights or benefits under the law. Adaw saw that the country offered no education for her children and little hope for the future. She decided to leave as soon as possible. "I went to the UN office to fill out the paper to be a refugee," Adaw said. "I tell them my husband is not here. They said, 'You are a pregnant lady with two children—how can you leave without your husband? It's very hard to do that.' So I call on the phone to Khartoum and beg my uncle to get Madut out of jail. He said he need to write an appeal."

A third boy, Aguir, was born in September 1999. Emanuel secured the release of Madut, who came to Cairo in 2000 and resumed his work as a peddler of clothes and fabric. He and Adaw got their own one-room apartment and waited on their refugee application, which went through UNHCR. The agency forwarded suitable applications to potential host countries, which had final say about who would be granted residency, an opportunity less than 1 percent of refugees worldwide received. Not long after the first World Refugee Day the United States approved their application. Adaw was pregnant again when they were summoned to the UN office in the summer of 2001.

"We know south Sudanese go to Australia and Canada and America, and we know that in all of those places they got a place to live and work," Adaw said. "So we just hope to go anywhere. "When they tell us America, oh my God, the excitement! You try to hold it in—you don't want to jump—but you are so excited! I call my uncle Emanuel in Khartoum and said, 'We go to America.' He got very excited. He said, 'Now you can go forward with your life.'"

Then their excitement gave way to alarm. They watched coverage of the September 11 terrorist attacks on a neighbor's television. When Adaw told Akoy that the attacks might cause their move to America to be postponed, he cried and told her, "I'm scared." Adaw became petrified of airplanes, though she hid it from her children. "I didn't eat for two days," Adaw said. "I call my uncle in Khartoum and said, 'I don't know if I'm going to die with my husband and children.' He prayed with me and said, 'Put that negativity out of your mind—pretend you are in a boat God made to cross the sea.'"

Security and safety concerns slowed the process to the point that U.S. refugee admissions dropped from 68,925 in 2001 to 26,788 in 2002. With their admission to the United States on hold, Adaw, Madut, and their two oldest boys, who spoke Dinka and Arabic, took an introductory class in English. The parents continued to work. When they left in the morning, six-year-old Akoy was in charge of his two brothers. "Keep the door locked until I get back; don't go downstairs," Adaw told him. When a parent returned home, Akoy rushed out to play soccer with neighborhood kids. Years later he carried a few memories of Cairo. One was the searing heat.

Another was the racist taunting of the Egyptian kids. He also remembered being hit by a "blue car or motorcycle" while on an errand for his mother. He wasn't hurt, he recalled, but he "cried a lot" until Adaw came and took him home.

Adaw gave birth to her daughter, Achol, in December 2001. The infant girl and her brothers, Maguy and Aguir, were baptized at All Saints Episcopal Cathedral, a haven for south Sudanese refugees. Finally, in early June 2002, the family got a green light from authorities. Adaw, Madut, and their four children boarded a plane for America.

"I got into the airplane and prayed," Adaw said. "I tell my kids they can eat, but I don't want to. I don't remember how many airplanes we rode but we got to New York, and from there we got to Baltimore. When our plane landed, I cried and said, 'Thank you Jesus; you got us here safe.' Adaw concludes, "We came off the airplane, and a [south] Sudanese man who wore a necktie greeted us in our language. His name was Joseph Madut Kuot; he was there to translate for us. He picked us up with other people from his church. We were exhausted but very excited. We were finally in America and safe. It was a great day."

First Thanksgiving

2

The Agaus' first home on American soil was in Westminster, Maryland, a town of 18,500, north and west of Baltimore. A local affiliate of the non-profit Church World Service (CWS) arranged social security numbers, housing, food, clothing, job counseling, and medical care for their first ninety days in the United States. Refugees could access a federal cash and medical assistance program for eight months.

CWS was founded in 1946 to help refugees of World War II. It proclaimed as its mission, "Feed the hungry, clothe the naked, heal the sick, comfort the aged, shelter the homeless." In 1976, with federal funding, it began to open refugee resettlement offices in twenty-one states.

The Agau family had the same needs and problems as nearly half a million refugees resettled by CWS since 1946. Refugees typically struggled with language, employment, discrimination, poverty, isolation, stereotyping, housing, concern for separated or lost family members, and parenting children in a new culture. Rules and bureaucracies were problematic.

"We have issues where people don't know the rules of apartments and don't know how to make payments," said Ryan Overfield of Lutheran Family Services of Nebraska, an affiliate of CWS. "In the developing world, particularly in refugee camps, there is a less formal economy. Western societies have faceless interactions with bureaucracies. Refugees are not used to that level of structure, to paying rent on time, putting garbage at a location. The list is endless. There are so many rules in Western society, and they've got to learn to play by the rules." A team of ten church members helped the Agaus with mail, haircuts, groceries, medical needs, and finances. One church member clipped photos from supermarket ads to create a shopping list for Adaw.

The Agaus lived in a motel for three months and then rented a house from a member of a local Baptist church aiding their resettlement. Akoy and Maguy were enrolled in the Carroll County school system for their first classroom experiences, while Aguir was enrolled in Head Start. Madut was hired by a local resettlement agency to bale and stack donated clothing, and on weekends he washed dishes at a restaurant. Adaw got a job filing and stacking in the warehouse of a book publisher. They alternated Sundays between Baptist and Catholic churches because the Baptist church offered Bible study, singing, and tutoring for the children, while the Catholic church made Adaw feel at home.

The south Sudanese man who had greeted them at the airport, Joseph, became a trusted companion and translator. Adaw and Madut enrolled in an English as a Second Language class in which Adaw progressed more quickly than her husband. Neither grasped English as quickly as their children, in particular Akoy, who was driven to fit in. Akoy cried when his second-grade teacher handed out a test to his classmates but told him he wasn't ready to take it. "I just didn't like that feeling, being secluded from everyone," Akoy recalled. He read children's books at home to hasten his learning and soon took on the role of translator for his parents. "He learned so fast and became a big help to us," Adaw said.

On a Maryland playground Akoy discovered basketball. At first he was indifferent to it. But as he dribbled and shot and bantered with the local kids, he changed his mind. At home he told his parents he liked the American game with the ball and hoop.

"That is not how you supposed to play," Adaw told him. "You supposed to play soccer."

"Mom, this is what they play here," Akoy said.

"Soccer is better."

"I like basketball."

Akoy played when he could, and for his eighth birthday, which fell on Thanksgiving Day 2002, the Baptist church gave him a basketball. Adaw roasted her first Thanksgiving turkey, seasoned it with curry, and was featured in a *Baltimore Sun* article under the headline "A Refugee Couple

Finds Much to Be Thankful For." In a photo Akoy hovered behind Adaw as she basted the turkey. Madut told the reporter, through an interpreter, "This is a free country, and I feel freedom and I feel peace. Nobody will attack me and hurt me here."

Winter came, and the Agaus experienced frigid temperatures and snow for the first time. "A lot of snow," Adaw said. "The children played in it— they liked it. We didn't like it. We put the heat up to 80. We said, 'We have to go somewhere else.'" They yearned for a warmer clime.

In the spring Adaw and Madut heard Manute Bol speak at a local college. The 7-foot-7-inch Bol had been Sudan's first NBA player and came from Turalei, in the northwest of south Sudan, about eighty-five miles on a dusty road from Madut's hometown of Gogrial. Born into a traditional and prosperous Dinka family in 1962, Bol tended cows as a youth and once killed a lion with a spear. He twice ran away from home to avoid ritual scarification of his head and the removal of six lower teeth but then gave in to appease his father. (As an adult in the United States he wore false teeth.)

Bol did not touch a basketball until he was seventeen, after which he played on teams in Wau and Khartoum and for the Sudanese national team. He was persuaded to come to the United States, where he put in one season at the University of Bridgeport, was taken by the Washington Bullets in the 1985 draft, and as a rookie set a record for blocked shots, averaging 5 per game, thanks to his fingertip-to-fingertip wingspan of 8 feet 6 inches. His NBA career spanned ten seasons with four teams. Limited on offense due to his skeletal two-hundred-pound frame, Bol specialized as a defender and twice led the NBA in blocked shots, ending his career with 2,086 block shots and 1,599 points—the only player with more blocks than points scored. For most of his career Bol was the tallest player ever in the NBA, until 1993, when the Bullets drafted Gheorghe Muresan, a Romanian who was a few centimeters taller.

Near the end of his NBA career Bol began to speak out against the Khartoum government. "If I were in Sudan right now I would be starving with the rest of my people," Bol said at an Oxfam America fundraiser in Washington. "I eat good food here in America and I go to sleep at night and then when I wake up in the morning I see something on TV and feel really terrible. There's nothing I can do. I have about seventy of my people right now homeless in the capital of Sudan. They have no place to go." After he retired in 1995, Bol immersed himself in humanitarian work for south Sudan and settled in Egypt.

Bol returned to south Sudan in 1998 and donated an estimated $3.5 million to a Dinka-led rebel group, lost money in business deals, and divorced his Dinka wife and mother of his four children. In south Sudan, where plural marriage is not uncommon, Bol married two younger women and had five more children.

Then Bol was invited by the Sudanese government to become the minister of sports and culture. Seeing it as an opportunity to advocate his people's interests to the Islamic government, Bol accepted. But once in Khartoum, he was told the job would not be his unless he renounced Christianity and converted to Islam. When he refused, the government seized his travel documents and detained him in Khartoum for three years, during which time his health deteriorated. He finally escaped after he paid a bribe, according to one account. Another version was that he went to the Khartoum airport in a calculated gamble that the government wouldn't stop him in front of BBC cameras and reporters.

In 2002 Bol was admitted to the United States as a religious refugee and settled in West Hartford, Connecticut. At that point Bol was almost destitute, and his rent was paid by a Catholic charity. To raise funds, he traded on his celebrity on the lecture circuit and as the world's tallest jockey, hockey player, and boxer. He was a sideshow with a smile on his face because the money was going to his people. When the Sudanese Army sent murderous Janjaweed militia on horseback to attack the Darfur region in 2003, Nicholas Kristof wrote in the *New York Times*, Bol "was one of the southern Sudanese who led the way in protesting the slaughter."

Bol suffered a broken neck in a car accident in 2004 and struggled to regain his mobility. Despite his financial and health problems, Bol's dream was to build coed multi-faith schools in which Christians in south Sudan studied alongside Muslims from northern Sudan. The first school was being built in Turalei when Bol died in June 2010 from complications of Stevens-Johnson Syndrome, a rare skin disease that came from medication he had received in Africa. A memorial service was held at the National Cathedral in Washington, where his body lay in a custom-built eight-foot casket. Bol was, Kristof wrote, "a moral giant who was unsurpassed in leveraging his fame on behalf of the neediest people on earth."

But on that April evening in 2003 Bol was in Maryland to raise funds. He spoke in Dinka and English and urged the refugees in the audience to work hard and to adopt good models of behavior so that Americans would respect them and admit more south Sudanese refugees. After the event at the college, Adaw and Madut were introduced to Bol. They talked about the strife at home and about Egypt, where Bol had lived after his retirement from basketball. They connected as refugees and parents. "We talked about the futures of our kids," Adaw recalled. That evening Adaw regaled Akoy with her account of meeting south Sudan's most famous athlete. She upgraded her opinion of basketball, and he gave Manute Bol a cherished place in his heart.

By spring Madut was dissatisfied with his job; he wanted work that paid more but was held back by his limited English. Then their friend Joseph told them about Omaha. Joseph's wife and three children already had moved to the Nebraska city on the Missouri River to join relatives. Omaha had a growing south Sudanese community of 3,000–4,000 refugees. There were jobs in meat processing that paid up to twelve dollars an hour and required minimal English. Housing costs were lower, and some south Sudanese actually had bought their own homes, which was Adaw's fantasy. The public schools were well regarded. Joseph told them he was moving to Omaha. "You should move to Omaha too," Joseph said.

Omaha was on the Agaus' radar when the third World Refugee Day was held in June 2003. It paid tribute to "Refugee Youth" between twelve and twenty-four, a group that accounted for about one-third of 20 million refugees worldwide. "A refugee's life is never an easy one, but it's especially tough on young people who are robbed of what should be the most formative, promising and exciting years of their lives," said Ruud Lubbers, UN high commissioner for refugees. "At a time when they should be full of hope and dreams for the future, they are instead faced with the harsh reality of displacement and deprivation. If refugee situations drag on for years with no political solution in sight, the enormous potential of whole generations can be lost in the dust of a forgotten camp. This is a real tragedy."

The long-term solutions, Lubbers said, were repatriation, integration in countries of first asylum, or resettlement to third countries. "We must also ensure that young refugees are given every opportunity possible to develop their potential through a stable environment free of exploitation, abuse or forced conscription; through education and skills training to prepare them for the future; through proper nutrition and health care; and through nurturing the family unit and ensuring that those who are alone get the special help and protection they deserve," Lubbers said.

World Refugee Day came and went, and soon enough Adaw and Madut decided to move to Omaha, in part because they believed it offered a better future for their children. "The children were happy in Maryland—they didn't want to leave," Adaw said. "Maguy used to say, 'Why we need to leave America now?' He thought Omaha was another country. We say to him, 'It's still America—just a different place. A better place.'"

The Agaus were blissfully unaware of Nebraska winters when their flight touched down in Omaha in August 2003. Their friend, Joseph, welcomed them. They started anew—again.

Street of Dreams **3**

In Omaha Akoy's family moved into Mason School Apartments, a nineteenth-century, two-and-a-half story Romanesque Revival fortress of brick with pressed metal ceilings and transom windows. The Mason, as it was known, was a Nebraska version of Hogwarts School of Witchcraft and Wizardry, minus the gothic spires. To Akoy, a fan of the Harry Potter series, this was a good thing. Harry Potter's wizardry was what Akoy needed to help his family and himself. Harry Potter's defense of "mudbloods," outcasts stigmatized by evil Lord Voldemort, was a kindness all refugees and immigrants needed.

The Mason had been an elementary school from 1888 to 1983 and was converted to residential housing in 1987. Its address on South Twenty-Fourth Street, on a depressed edge of downtown, connected Akoy's family to prior waves of immigrants and refugees. Twenty-Fourth Street was known as the "Street of Dreams" for its cherished place in Omaha's history and imagination. North Twenty-Fourth had beckoned Irish, Scandinavians, Germans, Jews, and Italians through the late nineteenth and early twentieth centuries and African Americans from the South after World War I. South Twenty-Fourth, a few miles down from the Mason, was close to Omaha's stockyards and meatpacking industry, which had attracted the Irish, Italians, Poles, Czechs, Germans, Lithuanians, and—after World War I—Mexicans. Central and South Americans came later.

In the 1970s public education "refugees" came to Twenty-Fourth Street when Omaha designated the Mason's south annex—when it was still a school—as a special education facility for troubled students. "We got the kids that other schools couldn't handle or didn't want," said Mabel Boyd, the school secretary from 1969 to 1983. "Some of them had terrible problems. Some were violent. They came to Mason for help."

Now south Sudanese refugees occupied one-third of the thirty-two residential units at the Mason, among which was the three-bedroom unit of Joseph and his family. "Joseph gave us one of his bedrooms; Akoy and Maguy stayed with some other south Sudanese in the building," Adaw said.

South Sudanese arrived in Omaha in the mid-1990s, some as secondary migrants from cities in New York, Minnesota, North and South Dakota, and Iowa that were too cold or expensive or lacked community support. Several churches provided necessities, while a nonprofit agency, Lutheran Family Services of Nebraska, assisted new refugees, although it had no services for secondary migrants until 2007. One of the early arrivals was Tor Kuet, who had spent two years in a Kenyan refugee camp and three years in South Dakota before he resettled in Omaha. A Seventh Day Adventist with an activist instinct, Kuet founded the nonprofit South Sudanese Community Association (SSCA) in 1997 for both new refugees and secondary migrants. Kuet organized volunteers to teach English and translate for courts, hospitals, human services, and housing, as well as to help with job interviews and applications.

Soon the SSCA, with a grant from the Ethiopian Community Development Council and federal Office of Refugee Resettlement, hired Sudanese caseworkers. A collaborative of service providers that included the SSCA formed the Omaha Refugee Task Force in 2000. Omaha Public Schools and City of Omaha Workforce Development offered assistance by 2001. Programs for health, parenting, and women were added as refugees from Burundi, Congo, Ethiopia, Liberia, and Somalia made their way to Omaha, though in fewer numbers than the south Sudanese. In late 2002 a program called Project Welcome, started by a Creighton theology professor, Joan Mueller, began to offer academic instruction and legal and dental services to south Sudanese in cooperation with Immaculate Conception Catholic Church in South Omaha.

The SSCA's on-site English and driving classes were the first services accessed by Adaw and Madut upon their arrival in Omaha. Madut was hired to cut and trim meat at the Tyson Foods plant, where Joseph worked, across the river in Council Bluffs, Iowa. Adaw was hired to clean rooms at a Hilton Hotel where Joseph's wife worked. Akoy and Maguy were enrolled in elementary school. Within a couple of months the Agaus rented their own three-bedroom apartment at the Mason—no. 207—for $700. Adaw and Madut worked opposite schedules so that one could be home with the kids, but when neither was home, Akoy, who turned nine that November, was in charge.

Adjacent to the Mason was a modest wood-frame Baptist church. Across the street was a Habitat for Humanity "ReStore" that sold used furniture, appliances, and building materials. Up the block on Leavenworth Avenue was the Four Aces convenience store. A bit further, at Twenty-Fifth and Farnam, was the south Sudanese commercial hub: a small restaurant and grocery; a few storefronts; and the Sudanese Center, a social club. The surrounding residential neighborhood, abandoned by the white middle class in the 1970s, was in various stages of blight and reclamation.

Akoy was drawn to a basketball court in the parking lot in front of the Baptist church. He joined the pickup games and met a south Sudanese boy, Tarir "Ty" Gatuoch, who lived at the Mason. The two squared off in one-on-one or two-on-two games, and Ty, who was older by three years and perhaps more, had the upper hand. "I used to beat him bad," Gatuoch said. "But he wanted to keep going no matter how many losses. He played against guys that were bigger and stronger, and he was competitive. He pushed me because he wouldn't quit."

Off the court Ty and Akoy struck up a friendship based on mutual needs. Akoy needed a big brother figure; Ty, a family. "I never had a mother; she died when I was young," Gatuoch said. "My dad wasn't around much. When I first met Akoy, we didn't have food at home. I would go to his place; his mother became my mother."

The Mason proved to be hospitable and nurturing. It opened a room with computers and internet where kids did homework and parents looked for jobs and filled out applications online. It built a new basketball court along

Twenty-Fourth Street that was an upgrade on the Baptist church court. The building manager set up a volleyball net and bought volleyballs. In cold weather Akoy and his pals—Ty, Mohammad, Bolus, and Sam—played soccer and football in the double-wide hallways laid with thin carpet—to the annoyance of parents. Murals and pastorals of African life brightened walls in the common area. Next door the Baptist church offered activities and classes and even arranged an excursion to Six Flags amusement park. Akoy had warm regard for the ministry of "Pastor Bob and Becky."

The Fourth World Refugee Day in June 2004, with a theme of "feel at home," was the first for the Agaus in Omaha. It was observed after Sudan's government unleashed Islamic militia, known as Janjaweed, in the Darfur region. The resultant massacre killed 30,000, left 300,000 more at risk of imminent death, left one million homeless, and forced 180,000 refugees to eastern Chad. Adaw was terrified for her mother and grandmother, who had remained in south Sudan, unwilling to leave. Madut worried about his brother in south Sudan. In Washington, Colin Powell said, "Today, together, we pledge to support and to protect the world refugees as they seek a new life, a better life. . . . We vow to help them 'feel at home' within the international family, within the international community." Alongside Powell was actress Angelina Jolie, who held the honorary title of UNHCR goodwill ambassador after her trips to Chad and other countries to help refugees. Jolie said, "If you've never met a refugee, you don't know what you are missing. They are some of the most amazing people you could ever meet. I continue to be in awe of their courageous spirit and their ability to go on despite the difficulties they face. It is that strength of spirit we celebrate today."

At a worship service at Omaha's First Lutheran Church, attended by about 120 south Sudanese, the Rev. Goanar Chol told the congregants to be proud of their dark skin. "Accept yourself as you are," Chol said. "God wants you as you are. If one body is not reconciled to itself, there can be no peace." In other words, "feel at home" in your skin.

If Omaha wasn't exactly home, its south Sudanese population now was estimated at six thousand, the majority of whom were from the Nuer tribe.

19

In September a crowd of south Sudanese gathered at Memorial Park in central Omaha to pray for an end to the crisis in Sudan. Those prayers were answered, sort of, when the Islamic government and rebel groups signed a peace accord in January 2005 that gave south Sudan autonomy and the promise of a popular vote for independence in 2011. Cautious hope replaced despair as south Sudan became Southern Sudan Autonomous Region and lower-case "south" was replaced with upper-case "South."

Adaw gave birth to Atong, her fifth child and second daughter, in December 2004. Adaw and Madut, with English honed at the SSCA, passed the Nebraska drivers' test. Adaw left the Hilton to cut meat at Tyson Foods, where Madut worked and the pay was higher—about eleven dollars an hour. They wielded sharp knives and wore protective gear to carve cattle that, in many parts of South Sudan, were slaughtered only for sacred occasions. The work was perilous: a South Sudanese woman would lose part of her right arm at a frozen foods plant in Council Bluffs in 2006. Bathroom breaks were limited. Repetitive stress and carpal tunnel injuries were common. Each workday Adaw and Madut stepped into a refrigerated room and were reminded of how far they were from semi-arid South Sudan. "It was so cold," Adaw said. "You work in a freezer for eight or nine hours. You come home shivering and put [the temperature] at 80 degrees, and you still cold. You take a shower in hot water, and you still cold."

Madut's knees grew swollen and painful from long shifts in the cold. Adaw wasn't as stoic. By now her English had improved to the point that she could apply for a wider range of jobs. She got hired in the mail room at First Data Corporation, which paid as much as Tyson Foods and was passably heated. She rewarded herself with her first car, a Honda Pilot. "The car change my life," Adaw said. "Now I can get to school, go shopping, get food, go to the doctor. It help a lot."

Adaw's enthusiasm was tempered when she learned that her great uncle, Emanuel Bol, had passed away in her hometown, Wau. She cried and told her children, "He was a good leader and father to us." Then she led them in the Lord's Prayer. More sadness came with the death of Joseph Madut

Kuot, the trusted friend who had lured them to Omaha and brought them to live in the Mason. "He had been sick a long time and didn't know it," Adaw said. But then Adaw's sister, Teresa, arrived in Omaha with her husband and four children, and Adaw's spirit revived.

World Refugee Day in June 2006 launched ninemillion.org, a campaign by the UNHCR to provide education and recreation for an estimated nine million refugee children. Globally film festivals, photo exhibitions, food bazaars, fashion shows, concerts, and sports marked the day, with an emphasis on soccer in a nod to the World Cup tournament in Germany. In the Hindu Kush mountain range of Pakistan, 2.6 million Afghan refugees were treated to a show of Afghan fashions, as well as Afghan cuisine, music, dances, arts, and crafts. Lutheran Family Services set up a mock refugee camp on the University of Nebraska at Omaha campus to help visitors understand the hardships of refugee life. The theme of the day was "hope" because as UN High Commissioner for Refugees Antonio Guterres said, "If there is one common trait among the tens of millions of refugees . . . it's the fact that despite losing everything they never give up hope. Each refugee has a different story, but collectively theirs is a story about the triumph of hope over despair."

Meanwhile, Akoy was in the midst of an education odyssey, the details of which have blurred in memory. Liberty Elementary, All Saints Catholic, Belle Ryan Elementary, Beveridge Magnet Middle, and Norris Middle were schools on his journey, and there may have been one or two others. Academics were not a problem; his temper was. All Saints Catholic expelled him for putting a chokehold on another South Sudanese student who had taunted him as a homosexual. Another school disciplined him after he harangued a teacher. "Akoy was the tall kid," Adaw said. "He was good at sports; other kids were jealous. They called him names. When he was upset, he would say what was in his heart; he would be honest. I would say to him, 'Honesty is good, but this is what you did, this is what you know, and this is how you want to act.'"

Adaw believed in Akoy's basic goodness. He and Ty had joined Boy Scouts, which as far as she knew was a force for good. She remembered when seven-year-old Akoy had grabbed his agitated two-year-old brother Aguir around his head to thwart a tantrum. "What are you doing?" Adaw had asked. "I don't want my brother to hit his head, so I grab him by the head and neck so he cannot get hurt," Akoy replied. "Because the head is everything. If you want to have a good life you cannot have your brain messed up."

Prophecy 4

In the seventh grade Akoy grew to 6-foot-6 and began to dunk. He played for Unity Stars in the Kellom Youth League in north Omaha, and word soon spread to high school coaches and to the "grassroots" basketball community that operated apart from the schools. Grassroots basketball ran spring-summer schedules to develop and showcase talent for colleges and shoe-and-apparel companies in search of the next Michael Jordan. Purists—such as NBA superstar Kobe Bryant—scorned the grassroots game because it was said to ignore fundamentals and elevate individual over team. But even critics could not deny that it filled the months between school seasons and kept kids, organizers, and recruiters off the streets. For the most part the Amateur Athletic Union (AAU) governed local, regional, and national competition. As grassroots ball expanded in the new millennium, so too did the summer leagues run by Omaha's high school coaches, to compete for influence and control.

Grassroots and high school coaches began to cruise South Twenty-Fourth Street hoping to catch sight of the young giant at the Mason court. If they timed it right, they might see one-on-one battles between Akoy and Ty Gatuoch, who now played for Gross Catholic High. They might even see Akoy go down against his shorter but stronger elder, which he did one afternoon. "I was backing him down and he just fell," Ty recalled. "He broke his hand. I was devastated; I thought he would never play basketball again. He went to get a cast on his hand, and his mom told him he had to quit basketball. But a couple of days later he was back playing again with the cast. He had to hide so his mom wouldn't see him." Adaw likely did not notice because she was busy with her sixth child and fourth son, Akol, born in March 2008.

In the summer of 2008, before Akoy entered eighth grade, Eric Behrens drove up South Twenty-Fourth past the Mason. Behrens was the coach of Omaha Central, which had won its third straight Class A championship in March. At thirty-three, Behrens didn't look much older than the high school kids he coached, but he was the father of the daughter and son who rode with him toward the Habitat for Humanity ReStore across the street. As Behrens told it, the action on the Mason court was the furthest thing from his mind, further even than that. He swore that what happened next was random luck, a megabucks ticket. He caught sight of Akoy, all 6-foot 6-inches of him, on the court.

Behrens hung a U-turn, pulled into the Mason parking lot, and introduced himself to Akoy.

"How old are you?"

"Thirteen."

"Where do you go to school?"

"Beveridge last year. I'm transferring to Norris."

"We practice at Norris occasionally. If you see us you can hang out."

"Thanks."

Akoy arrived on the basketball scene at a watershed moment. South Sudanese refugees had excelled in high school cross-country, track, and soccer, and a few had played football and basketball since the late 1990s. The autumn of 2007 brought the emergence of Omaha's first South Sudanese Division 1 (D-1) basketball prospect, Koang Doluony, a 6-foot-7, 180-pound forward for Bryan High. A strong summer showing on the AAU circuit had landed Doluony an offer from Indiana State, a D-1 school. Doluony had a stellar senior season at Bryan after he committed to Indiana State, earning second-team All-Metro and honorable mention All-State recognition. Ty knew Doluony through their participation with the same AAU team, Nebraska Bison. Akoy and Ty drew inspiration from Doluony's success on the court, as well as his intelligence and character.

From afar they admired a more luminous star. For the eighth World Refugee Day, in June 2008, the United Nations awarded the Humanitarian of the Year award to Luol Deng, a 6-foot-9 forward for the Chicago Bulls.

Deng was born in 1985 into a Dinka family in Wau, Adaw's hometown. He was four when his father, Aldo Deng, a government official, was briefly jailed. Upon his release Aldo Deng sent his nine children to Alexandria, Egypt, while he and his wife sought asylum in Europe. Deng and his siblings endured endemic racism in Egypt until they moved to London in 1994 to rejoin their parents after their father was granted asylum by the British government.

At fourteen Deng went to the Blair Academy prep school in New Jersey, made his mark in basketball, and became the second-ranked prospect behind LeBron James in the class of 2003. Deng played one season at Duke before the Phoenix Suns took him seventh overall in the 2004 draft and traded him to the Bulls. At nineteen he became the second south Sudanese to play in the NBA—after the much beloved Manute Bol—averaged 11.7 points per game, and made the All-Rookie first team. He steadily improved over the next three seasons, and in his rise to stardom, Deng remembered his refugee past. The UN award was based on his contribution to the ninemillion.org campaign to bring education and sports to refugee children.

In a public service announcement for the UN, Deng said, "After I heard the stories of 'ninemillion' helping refugees with education, sports and just a better life in general, that's what I always wanted to do. You never know how much you can change someone's life. Everybody can join in and make a difference. I guarantee you it's the best feeling."

Deng's fame alerted grassroots and high school coaches to a potential surge of South Sudanese talent. Akoy played for the eighth-grade team at Norris Middle School in 2008–9 and was "good but not dominant," as Behrens recalls. "You could tell he had a good skill level," Behrens said, though it was hard to be sure because, as he was a tall post player, his team had struggled to get the ball to him. He must have gotten it occasionally because in Ty's recollection, Akoy had "a hundred dunks" for his eighth-grade team.

Eighth graders must declare a high school in the spring. Coaches from four high schools—Central, South, Bryan, and Burke—had communicated their interest to Akoy. Adaw saw that Ty had transferred to Bryan as a junior and that Bryan had more South Sudanese than the other schools. "You're going to Bryan," she told Akoy.

Akoy was agreeable. He wanted to play alongside Ty for his friend's last year of varsity ball. Ty looked forward to having Akoy as a teammate. As they talked it over, Akoy voiced an idea—a fantasy—that made his friend chuckle.

"We can win state," Ty said. "I want one so bad."

"I want more than one," Akoy said.

"Okay."

"I want four."

"You crazy."

In eighth grade Akoy joined Team Nebraska, a grassroots AAU team that had corralled some of the best South Sudanese players, including Ty. It was Ty who introduced Akoy to Scott Hammer, Team Nebraska's coach. Hammer, married and father to one son, made his living as an insurance underwriter, but his passion and ambition were focused on his youth teams, ages 12–17. Akoy's refugee background contrasted with Hammer's upbringing on a farm in Wayne, Nebraska, yet the two bonded over basketball. Akoy found a mentor in Hammer, and Hammer found a talent to elevate the regional and national profile of Team Nebraska and, in the best possible scenario, attract a shoe-and-apparel company as a sponsor.

Through Team Nebraska Akoy experienced basketball for the first time on a national level. In the summer of 2009 Akoy played for Hammer's team in Iowa, South Dakota, Wisconsin, Illinois, Missouri, and Nevada. To put down a record of his travels, he began to use his Facebook page. Akoy had opened an account on Facebook in 2007, in seventh grade, and had listed his birthday as November 28, 1992, instead of 1994, to skirt the minimum age requirement of thirteen. Akoy made an initial post in August 2007 and then let his page lie fallow until 2009, by which time Facebook had three hundred million active users (on its way to two billion by 2017). Social networks, in 2009, were reshaping the world. The appeal was irresistible: a platform to build social capital, to tell life stories, and to be nosey. Athletes and teams were swept up in the excitement and used the access and transparency of social media to get closer to their fans.

But access and transparency were double-edged. The University of Texas booted a football player off its team for a racist post shortly after President Barack Obama's election in 2008. A Florida football player, who was white, was vilified after he joined a Facebook group called "Africa gives nothing to anyone—except AIDS." A Wake Forest football player was expelled after he used Facebook to warn students that he planned to blow up the campus and had an "uzi locked and loaded" for those left standing.

NFL teams began to troll social networks to gain insight into college prospects. At the University of Iowa an administrator began random checks on its athletes for social media violations that included nudity, sexual misconduct, underage alcohol consumption, use of illegal drugs, hazing and obscene gestures. Colleges began to lay down social network rules in their student-athlete handbooks. In September 2009 President Obama would talk to students at Wakefield High School in Arlington, Virginia, and advise them to "be careful about what you post on Facebook. . . . Whatever you do, it will be pulled up again later somewhere in your life."

In the summer of 2009 Akoy began to post on Facebook in fractured street dialect. "Just got back from Milwaukee and it's 5:30 a.m. in da morning," he wrote on July 14. The next day he added, "Back in Borin Ass Omaha Nebraska." On July 20 he wrote, "Fuck I might not be fuckin goin to Las Vegas tomorrow." Asked to explain, Akoy replied, "Cause my mom won't let me go." The next day he posted, "Im Goin 2 Vegas Im Goin 2 Vegas YEAAA." The next post, from Las Vegas, was, "Well I'm in Vegas with a lot of sexy women down here. I'ma move down here 1 day. And I found out my coach was talking 2 doc sandler about me." Kenneth "Doc" Sadler was the head coach at the University of Nebraska.

In Omaha Akoy played in a league of high school kids at the University of Nebraska–Omaha field house. Among its coaches was Bryan High's Tim Cannon. One afternoon after play had stopped, Cannon spoke to Akoy. "He made a comment that I wouldn't play varsity—that I was only good enough to play freshman," Akoy recalled. "I was a little offended." Akoy stormed out of the field house just as Hammer, who had hoped to catch Akoy in action, arrived.

"Let's go," Akoy said.

"Where are we going?"

"I can't play for this guy. I'm done."

"What happened?"

"I'm not going to Bryan. Not going to happen."

That's when Hammer realized, as he later put it, that Akoy had "some attitude and anger issues." Now he had to help Akoy choose another high school. Adaw favored two Catholic high schools, Creighton Prep and Gross, because religion was important to her. Akoy was religious too, but Hammer had told him, "Sunday is for religion; the rest of the week is for other stuff." There was South High, with its majority Latino student body. Several South Sudanese had played for South coach Bruce Chubick in a program that had had little success. Chubick had invited Akoy to his home, where he had met Chubick's wife Dianne. Later Dianne Chubick told her husband, "He's not coming to South. He doesn't have the courage." What she meant was that Akoy did not want to try to turn around her husband's struggling program. If her opinion seemed ungenerous, it was more of a statement on the bitterness some high school coaches held toward Hammer. Chubick referred to Hammer as a "street agent." "He's not very well liked in the coaching community," Chubick said. "Because of the shit he pulled with kids. He's not the only one. But he's probably the most notorious because where he pushed the kids, those schools had the most success. Maybe it's sour grapes that he didn't push any our way."

"They hate me," was how Hammer characterized his relationship with Omaha's high school coaches. "They hate me because what I do makes them look bad. They want to control their kids at school, but they don't put in the time that I do. They're educators and teachers. I'm a mentor. "When you're in the car for six hours with kids, you build relationships. They're going to trust you more."

Hammer had a collegial relationship with at least one high school coach, Eric Behrens, at Central. They had met as students at Wayne State College in the mid-1990s. Hammer already had sent Behrens numerous starters and several All-Metro players, Deverell Biggs the most recent. His players had helped Behrens win three straight state titles. Now Akoy sought Hammer's advice.

"Where should I go?"

"Take basketball out of the equation," Hammer said. "Where are your friends going to high school?"

"Most of them are going to Central."

"Well then you should go to Central. Those are four years of your life, and you want good memories."

One of Akoy's new friends at Team Nebraska was Biggs, who would be a senior at Central. Talented and temperamental, Biggs was someone with whom Akoy could identify and look up to. Biggs had urged Akoy to go to Central, and now Hammer did as well. Central was convenient, about ten blocks from the Mason.

"Okay then. Central," Akoy said. Hammer delivered the news to Behrens. "Until we get the paperwork, I'm out of this," Behrens said. "We didn't have this conversation."

Akoy posted about his decision early in August: "Goin 2 bed goin 2 da tac building tomorrow mornin 2 go transver." The TAC building was the administrative center where Akoy requested his transfer to Central. The next day, with the transfer approved, he wrote, "i am a superstar . . . the spotlight iz shining on me . . . and i am good enough . . . but she still doent love me."

When word reached Tim Cannon, he called Behrens and protested. Behrens thought it ironic because Cannon was perceived to have recruited Doluony away from Burke High. Cannon went to the Mason, found Akoy in the parking lot, and urged him to reconsider, but Akoy's mind was made up. "Hammer's influence was pretty clear," Cannon recalled. "He saw that Central didn't have a big guy, whereas we did."

Akoy called Behrens and asked what he should expect and how to prepare. In August, before school started, Behrens worked out Akoy at the Central gym. Behrens fed the ball to Akoy at the top of the key, where he faced up for fifteen-foot jumpers. He faked a shot, put it on the floor, dribbled twice, and exploded to the rim for a layup. Behrens went one-on-one with Akoy and observed him handle the ball, shoot, and attack the rim off the dribble. "He showed me a skill level I didn't know he had," Behrens recalled. "Right away I knew he was good. But I still didn't know how he would perform in a varsity game."

Akoy's confidence was not an issue—at least not outwardly. Before the start of school Akoy ran into Herb Welling, who had just quit as a volunteer assistant to Behrens. Welling was a grassroots "hoops whisperer," with a national reputation for innovative ideas about offense and with close connections to top college coaches and to the famed Five-Star Basketball Camp. He had been mentored by grassroots pioneer Rick Henkel in the early 1990s and in turn had mentored Hammer. Welling had decided to leave Central, where he had worked as a security guard, after the district had cracked down on his overtime submissions. A week earlier he had worked out Akoy at Hammer's request.

Akoy buttonholed Welling in the area outside Central's west entrance, which faced Joslyn Art Museum.

"I heard you're leaving," Akoy said. Welling nodded.

"You shouldn't."

"Why not?"

"Because we're going to win four."

"Four?"

"Straight."

Fantasy had become prophecy. It seemed far-fetched yet oddly plausible too. Central's assistant principal at the time, Edward Bennett, greeted ninth graders at the west steps on the first day of school. He saw Akoy walk up the steps and remarked to another staff member, "I think I just watched four state titles walk into the building."

Apparently Behrens had forgotten to alert school officials of Akoy's decision. When the athletic director, Darin Williams, saw Akoy enter the building, he rushed to his office and called district headquarters. "He told them we had not recruited Akoy away from another school at the last minute and that we were surprised to see him," Bennett recalled. "He wanted to make sure we were not accused of anything untoward."

A month into his freshman year Akoy received a letter that he posted about with glee: "FINALLY GOT MY FIRST LETTER 2 COLLEGE! ITS FROM RICE UNIVERSITY. YEA BABY!!! At this point he had not played a single minute of high school basketball. Rice had heard of him through a Houston-based grassroots coach who had seen him on the summer circuit. The letter, only an expression of interest, harkened a future of possibility. Two months into his freshman year Akoy put up a post that had nothing to do with basketball and everything to do with being a high school freshman: "MAN IM LONELY I NEED ME A GIRL. ANY OFFERS OR TAKERS?"

This post provoked a flurry of wisecracks from male friends, as well as one from Scott Hammer that touched a nerve: "You dont need anyone but your books!!!! go to bed!!! ps. I dare you to say something!" Akoy fired back, in full street mode: "shut up. damn Scott what ever. tarir fuck you. and quinn u funny. but i didnt want niggaz commetin on diz shit. i wanted girls not men!!" To which Hammer replied: "if he dont take care of business with the books all you will see him doing is handing out water to the freshman 'b' team. HEY WATERBOY! get me some fresh water."

Central   5

Akoy set out to make history, though he did not yet know it, at a school that dripped with history. Central was Omaha's first and oldest high school, founded in 1859, eight years before Nebraska became a state. Its impeccable French Renaissance Revival building went up between 1900 and 1912, on a hill above downtown and the Missouri River, and was added to the National Register of Historic Places in 1979. Its student newspaper, *The Register*, founded in 1886, had as its first assistant editor Victor Rosewater, whose father, Edward Rosewater, had telegraphed President Abraham Lincoln's Emancipation Proclamation to the nation in 1863. Victor later ran the *Omaha Bee*, a daily newspaper founded by his father that became notorious for yellow journalism.

Central was Omaha's "melting pot" school, acclaimed for diversity and academics. It graduated its first African American, Henry C. Curry, in 1876, or eighty-one years before another Central High, in Little Rock, Arkansas, integrated with the protection of federal troops. When Central's African-American Alumni Association formed in 1912, it counted forty-three black graduates and believed itself to be the only such organization in the country. Notable principals were J. G. Masters, who helped establish the National Honor Society in 1921; J. Arthur Nelson, who helped pioneer advanced placement for college credit in the 1950s; and Gaylord "Doc" Moller, who steadied the school through urban upheaval from 1968 to 1995.

A short list of accomplished alumni includes Nobel Prize winners Lawrence Klein and Alan Heeger, actor Henry Fonda and actress Dorothy McGuire, NFL running backs Gayle Sayers and Ahman Green, builder Peter Kiewit, publisher and civil rights activist Carlton Goodlett, educators Virginia Lee Pratt and W. Edward Clark, Medal of Honor recipient James

Fous, and advocate-for-the-disabled Jordan Somer. Five generations of Warren Buffett's family attended Central, though the "Oracle of Omaha" did not. His children, philanthropists and social activists Susie, Howard, and Peter Buffett, were alumni, as was their mother, the late Susan Thompson Buffett. Charles Munger, longtime business partner of Buffett, was an alumnus. High-achieving alumni dotted all walks of life. The nonprofit Central High Foundation, founded in 1997, had, in the idiom of basketball, a deep bench.

I was a 1969 graduate. In my time African American enrollment was 17 percent; it had run closer to 10 percent from the 1940s to the early 1960s. The majority was a mix of whites with pan-European roots, Catholic and Protestant. I was among the 20–25 percent who were Jewish. In the 1970s white enrollment began a slow decline while African American enrollment had risen to 30 percent by 1984. Latino enrollment began to rise in the 1970s and climbed above 10 percent in the new millennium. Asian Americans and Native Americans accounted for about 3 percent of 2,353 students in 2000.

Central's first south Sudanese refugees arrived in the late 1990s, with names that challenged teachers and classmates: Tut Chuol, Gatlunk Nyak, Sara Nyambok, Gatluak Nyak, Gatwech Tut, Nyaduer Jock, Nyanchiew Kuek, Dobuol Kueth, Gatong Gatluak and Lol Kuek. Most south Sudanese attended Bryan High and avoided Central due to the latter's sizeable African American cohort: relations between African immigrants and African Americans were strained for reasons rooted in culture and economics. "If you're new to a community with a high level of violence and I'm at the bottom of the ladder, my attitude is, 'You're coming to take my stuff,'" explained A'Jamal Byndon, a 1973 Central graduate and an instructor in the Department of Black Studies at the University of Nebraska–Omaha (UNO).

About twenty south Sudanese were counted at Central at the new millennium. Several had come over without parents or relatives. "The experiences they had in Sudan were atrocious; the things they had survived, they never forgot," recalled Linda Ganzel, who ran the ESL program. "Something would trigger their memory, and they would go back to that dark place. Some never talked about it; some did."

33

South Sudanese translators and liaisons were not provided in the first few years, so the teachers made do, often with the help of a semi-proficient student or two. The south Sudanese spoke Arabic and tribal languages. The boys had had some education in south Sudan, and their multilingual ability helped them learn English quickly. They also caught on to Spanish with their exposure to Latino students. But the girls had been kept at home in south Sudan and tended to have no reading or writing skills. "The girls were so eager to learn; they had an incredible thirst for knowledge," Ganzel said. "But you know you're in trouble when eighteen-year-old girls are holding a picture book upside down."

Four south Sudanese boys shared a one-bedroom apartment a couple of miles from Central at Thirty-Third and Burt. They held part-time jobs in the late afternoons, evenings, and sometimes overnight. They pooled their resources to meet expenses and came to Central each morning, sleep-deprived but determined to learn. One of those boys, Lol Kuek, made an impression on Ganzel on a frigid winter day. A new south Sudanese boy had come to school without a coat, boots, hat, gloves, or winter clothes. As the boy was about to leave, Lol took off his hat and coat and gave them to him. After the boy left, Ganzel tapped Lol on the shoulder.

"Do you have another hat and coat?" she asked.

"No, but it's okay," said Lol. "I remember my first year here, and I thought I would die."

Although faculty held a coat drive in the fall for refugee students, Ganzel had nothing at hand. She watched Lol walk out the door into an icy wind and was moved by his generosity. A friendship sprang up over time in which Ganzel, who had grown up on a dairy farm near Nebraska City, marveled at Lol's upbeat disposition.

"How come you're always so happy?" she finally asked him.

"Miss, you have no idea," Lol said. "It's safe here. Nobody is shooting at us, no bombs exploding. We have free education; I just have to get here. This is what my dad wanted me to do."

Lol, she would learn, had lived in a refugee camp in Ethiopia before he came to Omaha in June 1998. His parents had stayed behind. Lol's father was a farmer and a Presbyterian minister in the Upper Nile region near the border with Ethiopia. One day Lol came to school sad and subdued and read to Ganzel a letter from home. His father had boarded a bus for a town in Ethiopia where he could use a telephone to speak to Lol in Omaha. But unknown attackers, believed to be of the Anuak tribe, had ambushed the bus and murdered Lol's father. "He was devastated," Ganzel recalled. "So was I."

Student and teacher stood side by side, both awash in tears. The next day Lol was back at Central. His eyes were dry.

"Are you doing all right?" Ganzel asked.

"I thought about it all night," Lol said. "This is what my dad wanted me to do. He wanted me to do something to honor our people. I'm going to do that."

After his father's death Lol took a full-time job after school so that he could send money to his mother, who cared for his younger siblings at an Ethiopian refugee camp. Lol graduated from Central in 2002 and as a scholarship recipient enrolled in an Environmental Studies/Life Science program at UNO. Among his friends were the Kuon twins, Both and Duoth, and their older brother Miyong. Their father had sent them out of south Sudan while he had stayed behind to care for their mother and his multiple wives. Central's 2003 yearbook, or "O-Book" featured the twins, then sophomores, who played soccer and were active in several clubs. Miyong was a student at UNO and worked as an ESL paraprofessional at Central.

In October 2002 the Kuon twins were among sixteen Central ESL students who traveled across town to Benson High to hear a talk by hoops legend Manute Bol, who was in Omaha to raise funds for south Sudanese relief. The yearbook ran a photo of Bol signing a basketball for the twins. Ganzel told the O-Book, "I think we have a lot of education experiences for Latino kids, but very few specifically for the Sudanese." Another teacher, Marnie Best, said that ESL classrooms tended to provide more resources for Latino students than for south Sudanese and other non-Latino students. The 2004 O-Book reported the formation of the South Sudanese Club, sponsored by Miyong Kuon. The club's purpose, Kuon said, was to teach

35

south Sudanese students about American culture while not forgetting their native culture. The ESL curriculum for 2003–4, the yearbook reported, included English "for survival skills," basic reading, math, math essentials, social studies, and technology preparation. The Kuon twins and Miyong's wife, Nyajouk Kuon, graduated in 2005.

The racial mix, when Akoy arrived in 2009, was 44.2 percent Caucasian, 38.2 percent African American, 13.9 percent Hispanic, 2.2 percent Asian, and 1.5 percent Native American. About 10 percent were multiracial, though not recorded as such until the next year. Less than 1 percent was African. Students from low-income households, Akoy among them, accounted for 56.5 percent of the 2,359 students and got lunch for free or at a reduced cost. The racial/economic balance was coveted for education and social growth, but it was fragile. It had tipped toward non-white and low-income at vintage schools throughout the country, with adverse effects.

Akoy's introduction to Central began with his coach, Eric Behrens, who was virtually raised at the school. His father, Rick Behrens, grew up in Council Bluffs and played basketball against the 1968 Central squad known as "the Rhythm Boys." The racial divide that shaped the Rhythm Boys and Dwaine Dillard, their star African American center arrested in an inner-city riot in March 1968, rolled forward to touch Rick and Eric Behrens.

In the mid-1970s Rick Behrens began to teach and coach basketball at Tech High, whose alumni included sports stars Bob Gibson, Bob Boozer, and Johnny Rodgers. Tech was located on the edge of the Near North Side, the African American ghetto, and though it had once been racially and economically diverse, by the late 1960s it was mostly black and low-income. In 1973 the federal government sued Omaha for illegal segregation of its schools, and in 1975 an appellate court cited the "deterioration" of Tech among causes for its order to desegregate.

The order's unintended consequence was the flight of white families to western suburbs and private schooling that dramatically reduced enrollments in Omaha. Central saw its enrollment fall from 2,201 in 1975–76 to 1,674 in 1976–77 and to a low of 1,409 in 1979–80. Omaha concluded that it didn't need both Tech and Central, located a couple of miles apart, and for a while it threatened to close Central, whose building was older and in more need of repair. But even prior to the court order Central had mounted a campaign to save itself, led by Doc Moller and Susan Thompson Buffett, a 1950 graduate and the school's first-ever female class president. The Future Central Committee marketed Central to middle-class white families in an effort to preserve its racial and economic blend. Omaha Public Schools (OPS) superintendent Norbert Schuerman, in his nomination of Moller for a *Reader's Digest* educator award in 1989, wrote that Moller "worked diligently with the community, the parents, the students, the corporate entity, the school board and the central administration to bring about a $10 million renovation of the facility . . . [and] arranged an aggressive ninth grade recruitment package that allowed for school visitation for full days. He instituted both staff, parent and youth-to-youth contact."

Tech tried to market itself as well, but Central's effort was more successful, and in 1983 the city shut down Tech. Rick Behrens was one of the Tech teachers reassigned to Central. Longtime varsity basketball coach Jim Martin recruited Behrens to coach the sophomore team and then the junior varsity. Sometimes Behrens brought along a helper to practice, Eric, the eldest of his three sons. Eric filled in as ball boy and kept shot charts and stats at games. "I learned math by calculating free throw percentage," Eric recalled. Along the way, with his dad's help, Eric fashioned himself into a canny point guard. Eric enrolled at Central as a sophomore in 1989, as a transfer from Westside High. He played jayvee and a few varsity games as a sophomore. In 1990 Central named Rick Behrens as its new varsity coach. Eric started for his dad for two seasons, as a 5-foot-8 point guard, and as a senior in 1992 he set a school record with nine steals in a single game. "I enjoyed playing for my dad, but it's not the easiest thing to do," Eric later recalled.

After high school Eric played for a couple of junior colleges, then walked on at UNO but couldn't crack the lineup. After a stint at Wayne State College, where he met Hammer, he turned his focus toward a teaching degree at UNO and married Central alum Trish Rahaman. He worked for the Boys and Girls Club, where he had a close-up view of grassroots basketball, and helped Herb Welling coach an AAU team that included his younger brother, Ryan, to a championship. By the time Eric was hired in early 2000 to teach social studies at an Omaha middle school, he was the father of two. Later in 2000 he accepted his father's offer to coach the junior varsity at Central, while he continued to teach. With an eye to the future, Eric hosted a tournament for eighth graders and cultivated the next wave of talent.

After the 2001 season Rick Behrens stepped down. In eleven years as head coach he had won more often than not, but he had not liked to recruit talent and had failed to win a single state tournament game. When Rick retired, Eric went after the job and beat out three candidates with more experience. "Everybody thought Eric got the job because of his dad," Hammer recalled. "That might have been true a little bit, but with Eric being a Central alum, it made sense to me."

Eric Behrens was shrewd. He arranged Herb Welling a job as a security guard and made him a volunteer assistant, which gave him an instant pipeline into grassroots basketball. The district's open enrollment policy, which began in 1999 and gave students more choice in high school selection, began to funnel more talent to Central—for example, Karl White. A sparkling new gym, funded by a city bond issue, helped Behrens sell his program. In each of his first three years Behrens guided the Eagles to the state tournament, only to lose to Lincoln High, twice in overtime. In his fourth season he broke through and won a first-round game before an elimination loss. By his fifth season Behrens had not only attracted the best grassroots talent, he had refined his program and matured as a coach.

Behrens ran hard competitive practices at which he played with and against his players, stopping to critique and teach. He ran "open" gyms his players used when they did not have supervised practices and had them lift weights in the off-season. He led his players on endurance runs, the most grueling of which went from Central down to the Missouri River, across the Robert Kerrey pedestrian bridge into Iowa, and then back, with the last leg uphill to Twentieth and Dodge, about three and a half miles total. More often than not, he finished first.

He demanded his players be responsible and accountable. "If practice was at 9 a.m., Behrens had me stand by the door, staring at a clock," said Chad Burns, an assistant coach from 2001 to 2009. "If the kids weren't on time, we closed the door." Behrens's demeanor was casual and informal, so players found it natural to address him as "E. B." or "Eric." He was sensitive to his players' off-court problems, which meant that he often fed players who had no food at home; later on, in the case of two such players—Josh Bruning and Michael Partee—he and his wife became legal guardians. "He understood kids; he looked at them through the eyes of being a kid and player himself," Welling said. "He was a players' coach; the kids knew he would fight for them."

"We're brothers," Behrens would lecture. "You want to beat your brother at practice. At games brothers come together." Before games, as his players suited up, Behrens reminded them: "Play hard, play smart, and play together." On the court before tipoff and after timeouts, as they broke their huddle, Behrens and his players chanted, "One, Two, Three, Family!" "Eric got kids to buy in to playing for Central," recalled junior varsity coach Jay Landstrom. "He talked about putting 'we' before 'me.'"

Tactically Behrens paired a full-court press with the so-called "dribble-drive motion" offense. The dribble-drive, which Welling had copied from a college coach in California, spread the offense wide in the half court and set up the guards to "dribble and drive" to the basket. If the defense collapsed, the ball was kicked back to the perimeter for a three-point shot. If the press or dribble-drive were ineffective, Behrens called something else. He studied game film, scribbled Xs and Os, and was open to innovation. His half-time adjustments salvaged games. "In game situations he could think faster than any coach in the state," said Rod Mullen, who taught a popular African American history course at Central. "After we'd beat an opponent, on the bus ride back, he'd be talking about the next opponent. He had stacks of videos in his office."

Central won the state championship in 2006, its first in thirty-one years and just the fourth in its long history. Then it repeated in 2007 and 2008. Four players—Josh Jones, Chris Griffin, Ronnell Grixby, and Lorenzo Wilson—were in on all three championships. Jones holds a special place in the Central pantheon because he came back from open-heart surgery—replacement of a diseased valve—before his senior season to lead the 2008 squad. Wilson's father was Lawrence Wilson, a member of Central's 1975 state champions.

With success came media, which Behrens handled with understatement and aplomb. "He never said anything that could be misconstrued as arrogant or negative," said Tim Shipman, who taught AP Psychology at Central. "We'd hear or read the comments of other coaches and say, 'Eric would never have said that.' He never said the wrong thing."

It was after the third title in 2008 that Behrens spotted Akoy on the Mason court. At that point, as Welling recounted, "We knew every kid from cradle to eighth grade or [knew] somebody who knew them. If you dribbled the ball in town, we knew who you were. We knew who could play and who couldn't." Behrens's 2009 squad lost by a point in the district final, his first team to fall short of the state tournament. The 2009 squad had a talented scorer in junior Deverell Biggs, but it lacked a big man to guard the rim. Behrens thought Akoy might solve that problem as a freshman. Then again, as a freshman, he might not.

The *O-Book* for Akoy's first year included an ode to newcomers titled "Create the Legacy":

> As new students and staff enter the doors of Central High they give much consideration to how they will change the school. Whether it be showing their school spirit at all the football games or creating new clubs, everyone adds some quality or characteristic to the school. Students try to create their own legacy from maintaining a 4.0 to becoming senior class president to just being recognized in the hallways by their peers. We all have four years to create our own identity and to achieve our own idea of success. The paths we choose may lead us in different directions, but our goal is ultimately the same . . . to create our ideal legacy. So it's on that path that we start and at the unknown where it ends.

Akoy's legacy, then just a seed in his imagination, would add to Central's long and distinguished history. In the fall of 2009 the school celebrated its 150th anniversary with a tribute to its hallowed courtyard, which connects students to Nebraska's frontier heritage. The courtyard sits on the footprint of the territorial capitol, the seat of government from 1859 until Nebraska attained statehood in March 1867 and for nearly two years after. The courtyard was open to rain, snow, and pigeons until a translucent skylight covered it and a floor was laid in 1981. The school's history was put on display in artifacts, photos, and books. Food was served. Students mingled. Teachers and administrators hovered and chatted. Guests were entertained. Life unfolded. Caitlin Sorick wrote in the *O-Book*:

> The courtyard is more than just the lunch room in the center of the building or a gathering place for a group of friends before the tardy bells ring. It is a place where gossip can be spread, laughter and shouting is audible, clapping or whistling can be heard, or even friendships or possible enemies are established. . . . Multiple changes have taken place throughout . . . the courtyard's existence. The one thing that has remained the same are the brick walls that hold and carry countless memories and stories that are distributed and shared in the heart of the school.

Akoy made his way through the courtyard clamor and observed the rules of social engagement. One rule was to tiptoe carefully around the table occupied by Dominique McKinzie and Ed Vinson, two juniors on the basketball team. McKinzie, known as "Domo," was as cool as his favorite rap artists—B-Hamp and Pleasure P. Domo and Vinson carried on a stream of trash talk and banter. "They made fun of everybody and anybody," Akoy recalled. "Nobody sat at their table—everybody knew whose it was."

McKinzie and Vinson ported their act into the locker room when basketball began in November. As the sole freshman on a varsity with three sophomores, three juniors, and five seniors, Akoy was an easy target. He took it in stride because nobody was spared and because in social matters he was determined to control his temper and project an affable self-possession.

More troublesome was his tension with the team's best player, Deverell Biggs, a senior who was third-team All-Nebraska and second-team All-Metro as a junior. Over the summer Biggs had urged Akoy to come to Central, but now that Akoy wore the purple-and-white, his tone had changed. The senior had trust issues with the freshman. As the season got under way, their on-court chemistry threatened to make a mockery of "Four."

Trust

6

Eric Behrens called basketball a "trust game." By that he meant that its flow—spontaneous and fluid—required teammates to intuit and sense one another. Behrens's past teams were characterized by balance and distribution on offense, with shots and points spread among three or four players of roughly equal ability, knit by his gospel of trust.

This team was different in that Deverell Biggs was the singular talent, described by Behrens as the "alpha dog." At 6-foot-1 and 175 pounds, Biggs was athletic enough to be the reigning state high jump champion. As an underclassman on the championship teams of 2007 and 2008 he had been teased about his skinny legs, but he had defended the best player, Josh Jones, in practice. As a junior he had averaged 16.6 points with a flamboyance that once got him a technical foul for hanging on the rim after a putback dunk.

As a senior Biggs would average 21.1 points and bring a dominant personality to the locker room. "Deverell could be demanding of his teammates; he was really competitive," Behrens recalled. Junior varsity coach Jay Landstrom likened Biggs to NBA star Russell Westbrook. "He was a freak athlete, hard-headed and stubborn," Landstrom said. "He wanted to win at all cost."

To Biggs, Akoy was the new kid with a huge wingspan and a too healthy self-regard. Akoy didn't take it well when Behrens did not start him in the first three games. "I was pissed," Akoy recalled. Nor was he happy with his limited number of "touches" while the offense flowed through Biggs. "If Behrens doesn't give me the ball, I'm transferring," he told Hammer.

Biggs may have detected, or imagined, a bit of attitude in Akoy. He may have thought Akoy was slow to catch on to Behrens's system. "Early on Deverell would drop off nice passes and almost hit Akoy in the face,"

Landstrom said. "He got after Akoy." As Biggs later explained to the *Lincoln Journal Star*, "I told Akoy he had to watch big men to see how they played. He didn't have a passion for it."

The team lost its opener to Burke and its fifth game to Lincoln. Biggs pushed Akoy to raise his game, and by that he meant rebound and block shots. "Once Deverell knew a player was capable of doing something, he wanted it done all the time," Akoy recalled. "I may not block a shot, and he would be in my face: 'Akoy, block that shot.' He was a passionate guy; he didn't like to lose. Sometimes his tone was angry or he yelled." After Akoy made a crucial turnover, Biggs exploded, "You can't do that—what's the matter with you?"

Akoy struggled with the criticism. One evening Hammer received a call about Akoy from Behrens. "He texted me seventy-five times; he wants to know where to drop off his uniform because he's done," Behrens said. "He's mad because he probably missed a layup he should have made," Hammer replied. They both chuckled. "Well, I'm going to shut my phone off," Behrens said.

Behrens, for his part, saw Akoy improve with each game. His defense was ahead of his offense, in part because he was not yet strong enough to post up deep. Defensively he had a rare knack for blocking shots without fouling the shooter. "As soon as you saw him play in a game, you saw his impact in terms of blocking shots," Behrens recalled.

Behrens pulled Biggs aside for a talk. "He's a freshman and we need him, and you can't always beat up on him mentally," Behrens said. "If you're hurting his self-confidence, you're hurting our team. You're trying to win, but you're going about it too negative."

"He makes mistakes," Biggs said.

"Look, if we're going to be good, we need Akoy to be not only good but confident," Behrens said. "Even if he makes a mistake, we have to say, 'Don't worry about it; next time.' We have to be more positive."

Biggs's discontent erupted for all to see in a game in late January 2010. Central was favored against Millard North, but the opposing coach slowed the tempo to keep the score close. When Biggs got into foul trouble in the fourth quarter, Behrens yanked him, to his visible disgust. He and Behrens had a heated exchange, after which Biggs remained on the bench and Central lost by two points. Their argument carried into the locker room, in front of the team. "You'll end up playing at the YMCA," Behrens shouted as he slammed his hand into a water fountain. "Water started gushing—super hard," recalled Dominique McKinzie, who filled out the starting five with Josh Hackett and Sean McGary. "We didn't know if it was okay to laugh."

Behrens put Biggs through a punishing running regimen in practice and did not start him in the next game, which soured Biggs's mood. Afterward Biggs harangued the athletic director and was slapped with a one-hour suspension in the classroom of Rod Mullen, who taught African American history. Mullen took Biggs to task. "You can't make this all about you," Mullen said. "You're supposed be the leader of this team. Well, then, lead it."

Mullen's classroom featured a "Wall of Fame" with photos and clippings of Central's most successful athletes. Biggs pointed at the wall. "If we win state, does my picture go up?" Biggs asked.

"You can put up any picture you want," Mullen replied.

Biggs reconsidered. He knew he had to be a better leader to win state. He knew that wouldn't happen unless he and Akoy were on the same page. He knew that Akoy's defense and rebounding were luxuries that enabled him to gamble more on the press. He knew that Akoy's upbringing was every bit as hard as his with a single mother on the Near North Side. Whatever resentments and misgivings he may have had about Akoy, he locked away. "Something clicked in him," Behrens said.

From Akoy's perspective, Biggs "cooled down and we got rolling." They won five of their last six games after Biggs's meltdown. They blew through the districts and first round of state with minimal resistance. Fast forward to the state semifinal—the game that forever defines the chemistry between Biggs and Akoy. Their opponent, Lincoln Southeast, was led by Derrius Vick, a 6-foot-1 200-pounder whose first sport was football and who would go on to quarterback Ohio University. Southeast was 20–3 and had come to state on a roll.

As expected, the game was a struggle, marked by tenacious defense and numerous lead changes. Biggs carried Central with a career-best 35 points, including consecutive three-pointers that turned a 37–30 deficit into a 39–39 tie. "He might have hit four NBA threes in the third quarter," Behrens recalled. But when Vick sank a pair of free throws with 11.2 seconds to go, Southeast led 52–51.

Then it happened. Biggs took the inbounds pass and split two defenders in the backcourt. He darted across half court toward the basket. As he entered the lane, two defenders were in front of him and another at his left elbow. Biggs went up, and all three defenders lunged to mess up his shot. But the best offensive player in the state did not shoot. No, he flipped a soft pass to a teammate closing on the left side of the lane.

"I actually wasn't ready," Akoy recalled. "I was in position to rebound in case he missed. Next thing I know, the ball is coming to me." Akoy caught the pass and put it in—no rim, only net. In Behrens's words, he "put it up with a little touch." Central won 53–52. Akoy scored the winning basket on an assist from Biggs!

As pandemonium overtook the Central crowd, the meaning of the play sank in. Biggs summed it up best when he told a reporter, "I was trying to shoot the rock, but I saw Akoy. He was right there and I trust him."

Behrens saw it the same way. "I don't know if Deverell makes that pass the first game of the year," Behrens told me. "He scored 35 points, and he dished it off. Obviously he trusted Akoy at that point. And if Akoy misses, it was still the right play."

The stunning semifinal finish made Central's victory over Norfolk in the state final almost anticlimactic, except that Akoy's stat line—18 points, 15 rebounds, 9 blocks—stamped his passport to stardom and gave him his first ring.

In the ensuing days, weeks, and months, the game everybody talked about was Lincoln Southeast. Years later, when members of the 2010 team got together, they talked about the Southeast game—and the pass from Biggs to Akoy, senior to freshman, with trust.

"I still can't believe he passed me the ball," Akoy said.

Stardom

7

Stardom came to Akoy like the bolt of lightning on Harry Potter's forehead. He emerged in the spring of 2010 as the next big thing. ESPN named him to its Top 100 prospects list for the Class of 2013. The *Lincoln Journal Star* wrote that Akoy had "made a statement" and had been "mature beyond his years" in the state final. The *Omaha World-Herald*, Nebraska's largest newspaper, named him Honorable Mention Class A All-State and third-team All-Metro.

The *Central High Register* featured him in an article in which he told student reporter Daria Seaton, "I want basketball to take me to college." Akoy emphasized his diligence in conditioning and said his inspiration was NBA star LeBron James. Later in the spring the *O-Book* ran the same feature. Now when Akoy walked Central's wooden hallways, his head was up in the air—and not only because he was tall. As Behrens recalled, "There was a bit of ego, a little of 'I know everything.'"

That was how another teacher, Jen Stastny, sized up Akoy. He was in Stastny's PASS (Positively Affecting Student Success) class, which was a directed study hall for students who needed help. From the beginning Stastny had looked past Akoy's basketball persona. "I think I was one of the only people treating him like a kid," Stastny recalled. "He was a ninth grader but he was so huge, he didn't look like a ninth grader. And he wasn't being treated like one by a lot of people."

Stastny, who taught English, was "hard on Akoy" to focus him on his course work. After the state tournament, she doubled down. "He let it go to his head," Stastny recalled. "I talked to him about his big ego every day. He had senior girls following him around; it was gross. The girls were insufferable. They would stop by the PASS classroom to say hello to him. I would say, 'Go. Leave. Scram.' He was fifteen. They were eighteen."

Stastny insisted Akoy apply himself to his course work. "I'm with this girl," he would say. "I don't care," she would reply. "She goes. You study."

Akoy settled on one girl—Jessica Vorthmann, a freshman—and enjoyed the perks of celebrity. Life was good at home as well. His family had moved out of the Mason after more than six years and into its own two-story home with attached garage, located about a mile and a half north of Central, on the southern fringe of the Near North Side, the majority black neighborhood gripped by poverty and disinvestment. The tidy new house was on a street of new construction so that it appeared to be what it wasn't—a home in a quiet, middle-class neighborhood in the western suburbs. The nonprofit Habitat for Humanity had built the house and had helped Adaw and Madut finance it. Home ownership had been in Adaw's plan when she arrived in Omaha.

"At first they want to put us in a three-bedroom house," Adaw said. "But I said no; we need four bedrooms, and we got four bedrooms. "To me it was a dream. My uncle told me as a girl that one day I would be married and have a house. Now I am married and have a house. It was great."

Citizenship was the other part of Adaw's American Dream. The naturalization test given to all applicants had tripped her up once or twice, which only steeled her determination. Hammer's wife, Leisha, arranged for the mother of one of Hammer's players, Angela Lallman, a teacher in the Omaha system, to tutor Adaw. Their sessions stretched over three months in the summer of 2009. "I have to really study," said Adaw. "I learned about the Constitution and a lot of history. How many justices. How many representatives. How many states at first and then what happened. I have to ask the children for help with some of the words."

Adaw took the test at the field office of the U.S. Citizenship and Immigration Services near Eppley Airfield. "They give you a pen and a paper and you try to remember what you learned," Adaw said. This time she passed. Near the end of September 2009 she took the Naturalization Oath with Madut at her side. His English had not developed to where he could take the test, but he shared her pride in the moment. "That's when you say, 'Woohoo—I am an American!'" Adaw recalled. "So many people having freedom. You realize America have a lot of people when you see so many colors and languages at the ceremony: Italian, European, Sudanese, Arabian, Indian—like one hundred people. Everybody is hugging. . . . You are here, you have freedom, you can vote. You just cry. Even if you been here a long time, you cry tears of happiness. You feel like it's your country, like you belong here. You think, 'I have a life, I can work, and I don't feel afraid. My children can grow up in a positive way.'"

From a practical standpoint, now Adaw could return to South Sudan and see her mother without travel restrictions imposed on non-citizens. She didn't know when, but a visit seemed more plausible.

On the tenth World Refugee Day in June 2010 President Barack Obama cited the work of the late senator Edward M. Kennedy, who had died the prior August. Kennedy had spearheaded the Refugee Act of 1980, which created the federal Refugee Resettlement Program and codified into law the right to asylum for refugees. Kennedy's 1980 bill incorporated the UN definition of "refugee" and standardized resettlement services for all refugees admitted to the United States. The law provides for nonprofit agencies—Lutheran Immigration and Refugee Service and eight others—to assist the government in resettlement.

President Obama continued:

Refugees face daunting challenges in an unfamiliar society with new rules, new resources, and often a new language. Yet, in spite of all they have faced—harrowing acts of violence or devastation, flight across borders in search of aid and shelter, uncertain and often prolonged stays in camps, and travel to a strange country—refugees are survivors. Living in the United States presents an opportunity to move forward, one that countless refugees from all over the globe have embraced. Their remarkable determination to rebuild a brighter future after great adversity embodies our Nation's promise and spirit of boundless possibility.

The 1980 bill came after almost two hundred years of American ambivalence toward immigrants and refugees. Embedded in American culture and politics is a strain of xenophobia, or nativism, which elevates the interests of native-born or established inhabitants over those of immigrants. For most of America's history nativists have targeted a succession of newcomers, which included Irish, Germans, Chinese, Jews, Italians, East Europeans, Latinos, Southeast Asians, Middle Easterners, and Africans. Their modern-day ranks include white supremacists, neo-Nazis, and racists of all stripes.

The original U.S. Naturalization Law of 1790 limited citizenship to immigrants who were "free white" persons "of good character" and thus excluded Native Americans, slaves, free blacks, and Asians. The Chinese Exclusion Act of 1882 prohibited the immigration of Chinese laborers. The Emergency Quota Acts of 1921 and 1924 cut immigration by more than half and created a quota system that gave preference to northern Europeans.

During the 1930s and early 1940s, as hundreds of thousands of European Jews sought safe havens outside Nazi-occupied territory, the United States had no official refugee policy beyond the immigration procedure in the 1921 bill. In 1938, on the eve of World War II, two-thirds of Americans opposed the admission of refugees, including children, from Germany and Austria. President Franklin Roosevelt appeased American xenophobes and anti-Semites on immigration quotas and infamously stayed quiet while a 1939 bill to admit twenty thousand Jewish children died in Congress. The Holocaust killed millions of Jews before Roosevelt created the War Refugee Board in January 1944.

The Immigration and Nationality Act of 1952, an outgrowth of the Red Scare politics of Republican senator Joseph McCarthy, upheld the quotas of the 1921 bill. Sponsored by one of McCarthy's staunchest Republican allies, Senator Pat McCarron of Nevada, the 1952 bill was passed over the veto of President Harry Truman. It provided for deportation of immigrants and citizens suspected of subversion. In a speech before the Senate, McCarron stated the following:

I believe that this nation is the last hope of Western civilization and if this oasis of the world shall be overrun, perverted, contaminated or destroyed, then the last flickering light of humanity will be extinguished. I take no issue with those who would praise the contributions made to our society by people of many races, of varied creeds and colors. . . . However, we have in the United States today hard-core, indigestible blocs which have not become integrated into the American way of life, but which, on the contrary are its deadly enemies. Today, as never before, untold millions are storming our gates for admission and those gates are cracking under the strain. The solution of the problems of Europe and Asia will not come through a transplanting of those problems en masse to the United States.

It is no small irony that the facility that welcomes worldwide visitors to Las Vegas is McCarron International Airport.

America's immigrant and refugee history is not without compassion and generosity. The Displaced Persons Act of 1948 and the Refugee Relief Act of 1953 admitted more than four hundred thousand refugees. The Hungarian Refugee Act of 1956, Refugee-Escapee Act of 1957, and Cuban Adjustment Program of the 1960s admitted many "escapees" displaced by the Cold War. The Immigration and Nationality Act of 1965, promoted by Senator Kennedy, eliminated national origin, race, and ancestry as bases for immigration. Its long-term effect vastly increased the numbers of immigrants and the percentage of Hispanic immigrants. The fall of Saigon in 1975 and a totalitarian regime in Cambodia fed a new wave of refugees. In 1979 the Carter administration doubled the quota of refugees from Indochina to 14,000 a month, and over an eighteen-month period 232,000 arrived and resettled.

The so-called Sanctuary Movement of the early 1980s provided safe haven to Salvadorans and Guatemalans who fled murderous regimes but who were not classified as refugees by the Reagan administration. The movement started at Southside Presbyterian Church in Tucson, Arizona, and spread to more than five hundred congregations of various denominations who provided shelter, clothing, and legal advice to refugees.

The Refugee Act of 1980 empowered the president to designate which refugees, and how many, were to be admitted each year. Predictably the decision became political and contentious. Proponents of resettlement contended that it was compassionate and humanitarian and that it advanced U.S. foreign policy and national security interests with states and allies that hosted the majority of the world's refugees. Opponents couched their racial animus in economic rhetoric; they claimed that refugee resettlement burdened taxpayers, tilted the political scales to the left, and flooded the workplace with cheap labor—conspicuously in the meat-packing industry—that undercut native workers.

Obama authorized 80,000 refugees for fiscal year 2011, which was 20,000 fewer than proposed by the Refugee Council USA (RCUSA), the lobbying group for the resettlement agencies. But 80,000 were too many for Refugee Resettlement Watch, a nativist group, which contended that resettlement agencies lobbied for more refugees because their government subsidies increased. (Ultimately the United States admitted 56,424 refugees in fiscal 2011, down from just over 73,000 in fiscal 2010. Resettlement advocates cited stricter U.S. Homeland Security checks for the decline.)

Refugee resettlement found itself up against the sort of xenophobia provoked by the 2002 publication of Mary Pipher's *The Middle of Everywhere*, which celebrated the diversity of refugees in Lincoln, Nebraska. Pipher, a PhD in psychology, wrote the following:

> Lincoln has been described by disgruntled local and insensitive outsiders as the middle of nowhere, but now it can truthfully be called the middle of everywhere. We are a city of juxtapositions. Next to the old man in overalls selling sweet corn at the farmers' market, a Vietnamese couple sells long beans, bitter melons and fresh lemongrass. A Yemeni girl wearing a veil stands next to a football fan in his Big Red jacket. Beside McDonald's is a Vietnamese karaoke bar. Wagey Drug has a sign in the window that says "Tarjetas en Espanol se Venden Aqui." On the Fourth of July Asian lion dancers perform beside Nigerian drummers. . . . At our jazz concerts Vietnamese

families share benches with Kurdish and Somali families. When my neighbor plays a pickup basketball game in the park, he plays with Bosnian, Iranian, Nigerian and Latino players.

A critic of Pipher's book, Tom Andres, wrote:

Pipher interviews three Muslim brothers who are in tears describing how terribly American men treat American women, a sort of "mirror image" of how American men view Muslim men's treatment of Muslim women. Yes, it is undoubtedly painful for immigrants to live in a culture they see as sinful. What is completely lost on Pipher is that this is exactly why it has made sense historically for people of drastically different cultures to live in separate nations. . . .

Tragically, the very thing that Lincoln Nebraska was accused of being, it was not, but is now becoming. It was once the middle of a strong and cherished culture. It was at the very heart of somewhere. Now Pipher almost swoons when she describes the colorful "diversity" of a downtown park, with women in hijabs next to women in tank tops, and so on. But a nation is not a costume ball, nor is it a bizarre anthropological experiment. Only now is Lincoln becoming "the middle of nowhere."

Refugees tended to be "othered," along with undocumented immigrants—indeed, all immigrants—as newcomers who threatened the American way of life. Nativists clung to this view, even though demographics in America never had been static. Nativists felt their cause vindicated by an upsurge in immigrant gang activity and violence. On Easter Sunday 2010 a seventeen-year-old South Sudanese youth driving in north Omaha pointed a gun at an African American walking with an assault rifle. The South Sudanese youth was shot in the stomach and barely made it to a hospital. Police found out he was a member of the South Sudan Soldiers, a gang of mostly Nuer youth. After the shooting, law enforcement and security experts estimated that there were as few as three and as many as fourteen South Sudanese gangs in Omaha. Though the number of South Sudanese gang members was estimated at no more than 350, the gangs would earn a brief mention in the FBI's national gang threat assessment in 2011. Their emergence mirrored a historical pattern in which street gangs, driven by poverty and social dislocation, arose from virtually every immigrant and refugee population to arrive in the United States.

The upsurge in South Sudanese gangs had intrinsic causes, such as lax discipline by parents, school failure caused by placement above ability level, and an English fluency "gap" that enabled children to manipulate parents in encounters with teachers and police. Journalist Kathleen Massara wrote, "When young men's self-affirmation is coming from their peers, when the adults in their lives fail them, and when they move from a war torn country to a rundown neighborhood, then the conditions are ripe for mayhem."

Basketball ignored politics and walled off Akoy from gangs. That summer after his freshman year he played an AAU schedule with Hammer's Team Nebraska Express and the Martin Brothers' Iowa team at tournaments in Florida, Wisconsin, and Illinois. He was the youngest player ever to participate in the Metro Summer Basketball League for college players. "It's good for him to play with older guys," Behrens told a reporter. Akoy already held verbal offers from Nebraska, Creighton, Colorado State, Indiana State, New Mexico, and Marquette and had heard from Kansas, Texas, and Memphis, according to newspaper reports. Hammer took Akoy to a showcase camp in Chicago, where more college coaches saw him for the first time. A video of his highlights went up on YouTube.

Buoyed by his rising profile, on July 7, 2010, Akoy posted on Facebook, "What IS MY Destiny? Its Whatever I Want It TO Be!!!"
Comments followed:

KenDawg LeFlare: "akoy we all know your fukkin destiny, yo big ass goin to da nba"
Akoy Agau: "hahahahahhaaha. yall trippin man i really suck and got alot to work on!!!"

KenDawg LeFlare: "well yu better get to work and dnt let all dat height go to waist"

Sam Bongomin: "Aye akoy don't go to the NBA . . . let's go back to Africa and start are own dynasty!!!"

Akoy Agau: "kenny yeah you got a point! and samuel yeah we should just do that!"

Things were good until they weren't. Adaw was fired from her job at First Data due to chronic tardiness. "It was upsetting," she recalled. "I have my car and house and now nothing [with which] to pay them." To pick up the slack Madut took a better-paid job in Denison, Iowa, with Smithfield Farmland. The seventy-four-mile commute twice a day was too much, so Madut rented a room in Denison. A marriage fragile from staggered work schedules and refugee stress, Adaw recalled, became more tenuous. "He need that job or we lose the house," Adaw said. "I wanted to move there [to Denison], but Madut didn't want us to go there. He wanted the children here, and he would come on weekends. And then sometimes he work on weekends and can't come home."

Madut's absence was hard on his children as well as his wife. "The kids love their dad—they want their dad to be there for what they do," Adaw recalled. "I try to explain to them if we was in a village in Africa, your dad would not be there. He would go to work in the city, and you guys would be with me. And then I tell them to call your Dad on the phone. Talk to him and tell him how you feel and what you need, what you did good, and what you did bad. I try to do that, but it was hard. Adaw said that Akoy understood: "He miss his dad, but he knows his dad try to do his best and his mom try to be here with her children. I tell him just focus on your future. Your dad's dream is to work and feed his family. Your mom's dream is to have a car and a home. What is your dream?"

Akoy could not foretell his future, but basketball would be part of it, he was sure. From Adaw's vantage, basketball was a nice sport that had its time and place as long as it didn't interfere with Akoy's studies and sibling duties at home. And now that she was out of work, she urged him to find a job. "To help with the car," she told him. He could work a part-time job and help at home, and if basketball could fit into his schedule, so be it. But Akoy was almost sixteen, the age at which, in South Sudanese culture, young men assert sovereignty over women in their households. So Akoy enlisted Hammer to explain to Adaw how basketball could lead to a reward—an athletic scholarship and college education—far beyond that of a part-time job. "She had no idea any of this existed or what the opportunity was," Hammer recalled. Going forward, Adaw would be in and out of jobs, and when she had work, she would ease up on Akoy for a time. In pursuit of independence Akoy began to spend more time at Hammer's home in west Omaha, where hospitality was warm, meals were ample, and his father's absence not so keen a pain in his heart.

At the end of the summer Akoy was back at Central. A chance meeting with Denise Powers, who taught business education and sponsored the Future Business Leaders of America (FBLA) club, helped launch his sophomore year. Powers was assigned to monitor a hallway and exit at the end of each school day. Her exit happened to be where Akoy waited for his girlfriend, Jessica. Powers knew Akoy played basketball, but she wasn't much of a fan. She nodded at him for a few days, he nodded back, and then she struck up a conversation.

"What sort of activities interest you?" she asked.

"Basketball. That's it, pretty much."

Powers encouraged Akoy to broaden his interests and extolled the range of clubs and activities available at Central. She hyped her own club, FBLA, and suggested that Akoy join. He said he would think about it. Then he told Powers what was on his mind. "I need a signature," he said. "Something people will remember me by."

Powers knew that famous people sometimes were noted for a signature gesture—a clenched fist, victory sign, nod of the head—and she wondered if Akoy considered himself famous. She told him what she told the members of her FBLA club: "A handshake is good," she said. "People in business remember that."

Akoy said he would give the handshake a try. A couple of weeks later

Powers asked Akoy how the handshake had worked out. His shrug answered her question. She looked him up and down.

"You seem like a warm person," she said.

"I can be."

"Well then you just need to hug people."

Akoy gave it a try and liked it. A gentle hug from someone so large put people at ease. He liked it if people opened their arms and returned a hug. And if they didn't, he lightly enveloped them. A hug became his go-to greeting and signature, a tiller to navigate stardom.

To Absent Moms   8

Several of Akoy's teammates played football and brought to hoops a blue-collar toughness he admired. Some harbored a notion that Akoy was "soft," which stung his pride. To prove himself and perhaps to sample the autumn spotlight, Akoy went out for football. He did so, he told a reporter, against the advice of "basically the whole United States, actually, more like the whole world."

Eric Behrens liked football enough to work the chains for home games. He and chain captain Scott Wilson, who taught history by day, entertained one another with trivia contests as they moved up and down the sideline. "Friday night lights, best seat in the house, I loved it," Behrens said. He paid attention to how football coaches managed games for ideas he could coopt. He came to appreciate the toughness of football players. "Football players have a mentality, especially good ones," Behrens said. "They can't shy away from contact or be afraid of hitting. They fight through little injuries."

Plenty of good football players had played for Behrens. Shaun Prater (2007) made it to the NFL. Courtney Grixby (2004) and Mark LaFlore (2002) started at the University of Nebraska. Chris Griffin and Ronnell Grixby started for Central's 2007 football state championship team. Nate Prater (2005) and Brandon Gunn (2004) played D-1 football. But as much as Behrens enjoyed and respected football, he did not encourage Akoy. "I was always for guys playing football, but Akoy may have been the one exception," Behrens recalled. "[I] just really felt his future was in basketball, and he had a better chance of getting hurt than of helping Central win any football games. Plus, he wasn't really all that good at football."

Football had an obvious downside: broken bones and concussed brains. Akoy's favorite pro baller, LeBron James, had been a standout wide receiver at St. Vincent–St. Mary High in Akron. James's mother had taken out an insurance policy on him before his junior season of football and then persuaded him to drop it as a senior. With a potential billion-dollar basketball career at risk it made sense.

Nonetheless, Akoy was determined to play and made the junior varsity as a tight end and defensive end. "He was a big target to begin with and an even bigger target due to who he was," recalled Jay Ball, varsity football coach. They tried to put Akoy's height and long arms to use. His quarterback lobbed him high "fade" passes, and he lugged one in for a touchdown. He tried to disrupt opposing quarterbacks with his upraised arms. As Ball expected, he took some big hits and delivered a few. When the season ended, Ball said, "Akoy decided football was better to cheer for and that basketball was his deal. I appreciated him coming out and his basketball coaches not getting in his way."

To Behrens's relief Akoy was in one piece when basketball started in November. But for reasons buried and/or forgotten, they clashed, not for the first time or last, and Behrens kicked Akoy out of the gym. This clash was special in that Akoy made it public on Facebook, in a manner that suggested he had taken too many hits on the gridiron: "news for the world! Akoy agau has just been put on the reserve team this year!! You probably might not believe me! But i am!!!!!!!!!!!" The next post, a day later, stated: "everyone i was just playing about being on reserve!!!" It was followed by: "hahahahhahahaaha everybody at school fell for it. and they said they was going to kill my coach. lol"

Imagination boggles at what must have transpired privately between Behrens and Akoy. Within a couple of days Akoy oozed contrition: "dear everybody, i sincerely apologize for my imature actions and language i have used on here. I also want to say sorry for all the kids that may see me as a role model to see me behave and use such inapropriate language. To my teammates, coaches, friends, and centarl high school i have let you down and hopefully somehow i can make it up to you."

After that he dropped a bombshell: "i will try my best to improve and make myself a better person and leader. I hope you will still see me as the same person you once saw me as. As far as basketball i will no longer be playing as of right now. Thank you and i hope you can find room in your heart to forgive." To the Facebook world it appeared as if Akoy had retired. And then, just before Thanksgiving: "Im going back!!!"

Whatever the issue, Akoy was back in the fold, ever more seduced by, and perhaps respectful of, social media. Notably absent from his posts was "gangsta" street dialect. Years later, Akoy recalled the episode: "One thing Behrens never allowed was disrespectful behavior. If I was out of line, he was quick to settle me down. At the time I thought he was crazy, but it was good for me; it kept me grounded."

After he had dealt with Akoy, Behrens assessed his talent with a gimlet eye: he had no Deverell Biggs who could average 21.1 points or pop for 35 in a state championship game. No, this team would have to defend the title with a different approach. This was a blue-collar team. Seniors Paulino Gomez (linebacker) and Ed Vinson (defensive end) were also co-captains of varsity football. Dom McKinzie and Calvin McCoy, the other two seniors, also played varsity football. Tra-Deon Hollins, Darian Barrientos-Jackson, Cameron Payne, Mike Welch, Deandre Hollins-Johnson, Deshun Roberts— all were football players. And now Akoy. "We had some really tough kids," Behrens said.

Gomez and Vinson, both of whom had come off the bench the prior season, were especially kick-ass. Akoy respected both because in practice he banged against their muscular frames. Gomez in particular was a kindred spirit. His parents had come from Mexico separately, in the early 1980s, and had arrived in California without documents. "My mom was very pale skinned, with reddish-brown hair," Gomez said. "In those days you could go through and say you were an American citizen, and if you looked Caucasian, they let you through. My dad came inside a suitcase, in a car."

Gomez's mother, Victoria Edwards, first married an American, which allowed her to be naturalized. His father, Paulino Sr., had become a citizen through an amnesty program. After Victoria's marriage broke apart, they met in Pasadena and became a couple. In the early 1990s Victoria and Paulino Sr. settled in Omaha, where she worked as a waitress and he worked in construction. Gomez was born in 1993, the last of his mother's five children. He grew up at Thirty-Second and Pacific, at the edge of South Omaha, in a neighborhood with a strong Latino presence. Many of the Latino kids he knew in elementary and middle school went to South High, which had the most Latino students in the city. But Gomez chose Central, he recalled, "because I was a kid who wanted to go my own path."

Gomez played soccer, football, and basketball at Central and was appreciated by coaches and teammates for his grit, savvy, and work ethic, if not raw talent. Gomez thought of his coaches and teammates as family, all the more so when his mother was diagnosed with brain cancer in January 2010, during his junior season of basketball. In March, a few days after Central won the title and Gomez had a gold medal hung around his neck, Victoria Edwards died at age fifty. "I wanted to make her proud; being on the basketball team definitely did," Gomez recalled.

Both the basketball and football coaching staffs attended the funeral. Behrens's wife, Trish, sent dinner to the Gomez home. An assistant coach, Ben Holling, gathered donations for a Wal-Mart gift card. When Holling came by to deliver the card, he asked Gomez how he felt. "I said fine; I'm tough; I can take it," Gomez recalled. "He said it was okay if I wanted to cry. So I did. That moment sticks with me."

Gomez's teammates buoyed him, none more than Vinson. It had been a year since Vinson's mother, Sherry Zollicoffer, had died from stomach cancer. Vinson had watched helplessly as her illness progressed; she was the sole parent in the lives of him and his three siblings. "It was a crazy time in my life," Vinson recalled. "What I remember is how Behrens and everybody on the staff supported me. Behrens let me stay at his house a couple times to get away from the stuff at home; he really looked out for me. That was huge to me at that time, one of the reasons I stayed in school." When Gomez's mother died, Vinson was there for him. "I reached out to him as a friend and a brother," Vinson recalled. "I was somebody he could talk to when he needed to talk. When I went through it, I didn't know a lot. When he went through it, I tried to help him make something positive of it. I gave him encouragement, and he did the rest."

Gomez did not show up much in the box scores and accounts of the 2010–11 season, but his presence was felt in the results. Absent a big scorer, Behrens built the team for defense and featured a full-court press and half-court zone trap. At guard were sophomore cousins, Hollins and Hollins-Johnson, who put relentless pressure on the ball after they became starters midway through the season. Defending behind them was a foursome who shared time—Barrientos-Jackson, McKinzie, Welch, and Vinson—all football players and bruisers. The last line of defense was Akoy, who had 52 blocks in 26 games prior to the state tournament. Even as Akoy protected the rim, his numbers improved from just less than 6 points and 6 rebounds as a freshman to 10.6 points and 6.4 rebounds.

Gomez, at 6-foot-2 and 200 pounds, got about six minutes a game, usually to spell Vinson or McKinzie at power forward. When he wasn't in the game, he made sure his teammates were. "I knew all the plays the other teams would run; I liked the Xs and Os in basketball," Gomez recalled. "I would yell at my teammates, like I was another coach on the bench. In practice I was good at being the scout team. We played teams that ran the 'flex' offense, and I was able to do that."

In practice Gomez often drew Akoy as his assignment. "I would always try to put a body on him to make him tougher," Gomez said. "I boxed him out and made him work." As the season progressed and Akoy's game matured, Gomez took personal satisfaction. He had known Akoy as a gawky middle school hopeful and had watched him grow and gain confidence. They shared basketball and the immigrant struggle. "We related," Gomez recalled. "My parents weren't refugees, but if you think about it, they left Mexico for a better life, not only for themselves but for their kids. Same with Akoy's family."

To reach state, Central beat Lincoln East 95–44 in the district semifinal and Grand Island 74–43 in the district finals. At that point the Eagles were 23–3 and had given up fewer than 40 points in five games and fewer than 50 points in 16 games, compared with having done so in 17 games in the previous five seasons combined. Only one of the championship teams from

2006–8 had held more than one opponent under 50: the 2007–8 team had done it four times.

The Eagles held their first-round opponent at state, Lincoln North Star, to 6 points in the first quarter and 4 points in the third quarter and won, 69–34. In a 70–59 semifinal victory over Norfolk Akoy had 11 points, 10 rebounds, and 10 blocks.

In the final the team drew Omaha Bryan, the school from which Akoy had withdrawn his freshman commitment and whose front line featured 6-foot-4 Reath Jiech, another South Sudanese refugee. Bryan ran a "flex" offense with a lot of back screens and motion. Gomez knew the "flex" schematic and helped his teammates prepare against it, though he was unlikely to see action.

Before the game Behrens exhorted his team in a locker room talk captured on video by assistant coach Jay Landstrom: "We're still hungry, okay? We've got to come out here in the first three minutes, and we've got to punch people in the mouth. Central's been good because we don't play not to lose; we play to win, okay? When we see an opportunity to attack, we attack . . . and we're not on our heels playing scared, hoping they make a mistake, okay? We make plays." At that, players huddled around Behrens with their fists in the air, touching. "All year, you guys have put 'we' before 'me,'" Behrens continued. "You've just wanted to win for Central. One more time I'm asking you to take that mentality out there." Together they chanted, "One, Two, Three, Family!"

Central scored the first nine points and led 26–16 at halftime. Bryan came to within a point, 46–45, with 3:43 left, and then came up empty on its next four single-shot possessions, which featured a crucial block by Akoy. Central made 6 free throws, with 2 from Akoy, and the final 2 from Hollins with 17 seconds left. Final score: Central, 52–48. Bryan was held to 27 percent shooting (12 of 45) in the eighteenth game in which Central held an opponent under 50.

Central won its fifteenth straight at state, dating back to 2006, and its fifth championship in six years. Akoy finished with 11 points, 7 rebounds, and 7 blocks, and he told a reporter, "I think we can come back and do

63

this the next two years." In the postgame locker room, again captured on video by Landstrom, Behrens praised his players: "I'm proud of this group because you found a different way to do it. . . . We held our last opponent under 50 points again. So you did it on defense. And it wasn't that pretty."

Then Behrens named his four seniors—McKinzie, McCoy, Vinson, and Gomez—and tapped his heart. "You guys know how I feel about you," he said. "I couldn't be prouder of you guys. I'm going to miss you, but I could not be happier that you got another championship in your last game. This one was for you guys—this was for the four seniors." Behrens raised his fist for the "family" chant. His players encircled, raised cups of water, and drenched him. Hilarity ensued, with Akoy, Gomez, and Vinson in the middle of it.

The highlight video runs just over twenty-seven minutes. At 23:21 it goes tight on Gomez, with a huge grin on his face: "We did it baby. We did it." At 24:20 Gomez, Vinson, and a few others bust a move to T.I.'s "On Top of the World." At 26:23 the camera finds Gomez and Vinson in front of a locker as they display their gold medals and linger for the last time in their purple-and-white.

"See this," says Gomez.

"That's hard work," says Vinson.

"Hard work," Gomez says. "Fifteen games in a row we've won here. That's cold."

"True Faith and Allegiance" 9

That spring Akoy fell in love with somebody other than himself. He shared a math class with a freshman girl, Lauren Wegner, whom he friended on Facebook. Wegner played on a select softball team with Charlotte Sjulin, a sophomore at small, private Concordia High in west Omaha. Through Wegner, Akoy and Sjulin, known as "Lotte," became Facebook friends. Then they became real-life friends. Then it got interesting.

"First time we met was at a movie," Lotte recalled. "Me and my two girlfriends and he and his best guy friend. I wouldn't call it a date. Just hanging out." An elite athlete in her own right, Lotte knew of Akoy's basketball celebrity. She decided to preempt his ego. "You can't sit by me," she told him. Miffed or pretending to be, Akoy sat three rows in front of the group. "So I knew it was going to be pretty light and relaxed," Lotte recalled. "And then he came back and sat with us."

To the naked eye they seemed an unlikely pair, she a luminous brunette beauty, the daughter of two physicians Midwestern-born and bred. She lived on 180th Street in an affluent west Omaha zip code almost as different from the Near North Side as from South Sudan. Race and class were vast chasms they stared across. Less obvious was their shared faith. The mission of Lotte's high school, part of Lutheran Schools of Omaha, was "to prepare young people for lives of faith, service and leadership as Christian disciples." Akoy believed in Jesus too, as a Catholic, and spoke openly of his faith. They jousted over the relative merits of the Catholic and Lutheran theologies. It was both good-natured and serious, and it carved out a basis for their mutual respect. Then too, as noted, Lutheran Immigration and Refugee Service was one of nine resettlement agencies for the U.S. government. Refugees were in the heart and soul of Lutherans.

Lotte was smitten. "The minute she met Akoy, she said, 'You have to meet this guy—he's super cool,'" recalled Ann Sjulin, Lotte's mother.

Lotte's father, Dave, was dubious. "I had seen him interviewed on TV, and he was kind of a character," Dave recalled. "Lotte said, 'I know Akoy; I talk to him all the time.' I said, 'How's that?' She said she was his friend on Facebook. And I said, 'You and a thousand others are his friend on Facebook. Everybody wants to be friends with Akoy on Facebook.' So I didn't think it was real at all."

Akoy's introduction to the Sjulins was delayed almost permanently. In April 2011 he was with three friends from Central—on their way to an afternoon track meet—when their car ran a stop sign about two blocks from Akoy's home. The front passenger side, where Akoy rode, took a direct hit. "We flew and hit somebody's garage," Akoy recalled. "My whole door was destroyed. I don't remember how, but somehow I managed to climb out on the driver's side." Police found Akoy on a lawn, bleeding from a head laceration. He assured them he was not in pain and could walk on his own, but when he tried, he fell in a heap. An ambulance took him to St. Joseph's Hospital, where he was diagnosed with a concussion but no broken bones. One of Akoy's friends suffered a broken wrist and another a broken collar bone.

This was not Akoy's first crash. The previous November he, Adaw, and her brother Martin were hit on their way to Wal-Mart for Black Friday. Nobody was hospitalized, but Akoy had neck and back pain for several days. After the more recent crash Akoy was hospitalized for almost a week. South Sudanese friends visited and laid crosses around his bed. One hospital worker gave him a blanket that pictured dollar bills above a message: "Get Up and Make That Money." Among the cards and flowers that came to him was a bouquet from Lotte and her older sister Lucy. On Easter Sunday, as the Sjulins drove back from a weekend with Ann's parents in western Nebraska, Lotte called Akoy. They chatted and then Lotte handed her phone to her father.

"Hello, this is Dave."

"Hello, Dr. Sjulin. I'm going to marry your daughter."

"What!"

Dave Sjulin managed to keep the car on the road as he relayed Akoy's "hello" to his wife, Lotte, and her two sisters. All were incredulous. "We're like, 'Who is this?'" recalled Ann. "And 'You're crazy.'"

The phone conversation continued for the better part of two hours as the Sjulins crossed the state. The snippet that lodged in Dave's memory was Akoy's question, "What do you like to bake?" Dave allowed that he made a "mean banana bread." Akoy asked Dave to bring him one in the hospital.

"So we got back from Easter and Lotte said, 'I'm going to take Akoy and his family some banana bread,'" Ann recalled. "Lotte never had an interest in cooking, but she and Dave made some banana bread." Lotte delivered banana bread to Akoy at the hospital.

Akoy asked to be released from the hospital a day early because he had an appointment to keep. His head was bandaged when Adaw and Madut picked him up and drove with him and his younger siblings (Maguy, Aguir, and Achol) to the immigration center near the airport. He and his siblings became American citizens that day in April 2011. Their test was waived under a provision for children under eighteen if a parent had passed the test. Absent a test, they could relax. On a video President Obama congratulated them and welcomed them to the responsibilities of citizenship. Alongside other immigrants and refugees, the Agau kids raised their hands and took the Naturalization Oath:

> I hereby declare, on oath, that I absolutely and entirely renounce and abjure all allegiance and fidelity to any foreign prince, potentate, state, or sovereignty, of whom or which I have heretofore been a subject or citizen; that I will support and defend the Constitution and laws of the United States of America against all enemies, foreign and domestic; that I will bear true faith and allegiance to the same; that I will bear arms on behalf of the United States when required by the law; that I will perform noncombatant service in the Armed Forces of the United States when required by the law; that I will perform work of national importance under civilian direction when required by the law; and

that I take this obligation freely, without any mental reservation or purpose of evasion; so help me God.

One by one their names were called, and they were handed their certificates of citizenship. One of Akoy's friends from grassroots basketball, Mike Sautter, snapped a photo of the four siblings. Adaw watched with tearful eyes and hugged each of her children. Then they went home to a party with family and friends. Adaw's sister cooked a couple of traditional South Sudanese meat-and-vegetable dishes. Fried chicken, a favorite of Akoy's, was served. That afternoon Adaw savored the happiness on the face of her oldest son. A day ago he had been in a hospital bed. Now he was eating fried chicken as an American citizen. He noticed her gaze and was grateful. "Thank you mom for bringing us here," he told her. "And thank you for helping us to do it easy."

The next day Akoy asked Lotte to bring, as she recalled, "Fourteen dollars' worth of McDonald's. An Angus burger with large fries, large drink, two McDevils, two cinnamon twists." But she got lost looking for his home because she had never been to that part of town. "She called me and said, 'I don't know where this is,'" recalled Ann. "And I didn't know because at that time I hadn't been down there either."

Akoy's citizenship coincided with a separate legal action in which Hammer became his co-guardian, with Adaw's consent. Hammer's rationale, with which Adaw agreed, was that Hammer was better equipped to deal with the onslaught of college recruiters and with Akoy's basketball future. Adaw trusted Hammer and took his offer to be co-guardian as genuine and heartfelt. "Scott was like a big brother to Akoy," she said. Behrens was skeptical. "I had players who really needed help. That wasn't Akoy. He had two parents who were concerned. Maybe they didn't know exactly what he was up to or what he needed—that was the cultural gap—but they gave him a home. Lots of people want to help the star players. But we had fifty kids in our program, and a lot of them needed help more than Akoy."

Near the end of May, Akoy showed up at the Sjulin's sumptuous west Omaha home for Lucy's high school graduation party. Akoy still had a girlfriend at the time. "Lotte, you need to back off," Ann said. Lotte replied: "We're just talking—it's no big deal."

Akoy was in the role of Eliza Doolittle. He wore his favorite Hawaiian red shorts and had his hair picked out. He declined Ann's offer of food and took a seat on the couch. "He sat on the couch the whole time and wouldn't hardly look around," Ann recalled. "He was totally freaked out because we didn't know him." "Yeah, I was scared," Akoy recalled.

Akoy's growth owed much to his fluency in English, the first beachhead for refugees and immigrants in America. They need it to figure out what to do, where to go, and how to be. Sometimes they need it to summon police.

In January 2011, as Akoy advanced upon his second championship, the primacy of language played out at the public housing project where Adaw's sister lived. A Somali Bantu refugee who lived at the Southside Terrace Apartments was mugged and beaten. The victim's call to police was ineffectual due to language difficulties. The assault had been preceded by a series of attacks on Somali Bantus in which the victims deemed police response inadequate. Now more than one hundred Somali Bantus gathered in frustrated but peaceful protest and asked the city for more police interpreters, more summer school programs for their children, and more ESL programs for parents.

The request for ESL instruction was particularly dire. An anecdote was told of a Somali mother who asked her son to go upstairs and bring down her purse. The son went upstairs and came back without the purse. "You disobeyed," the mother scolded. "Mom, I don't know what you're asking me," he said.

The argument escalated until a Somali elder was summoned to mediate. Among officials who listened was Susan Mayberger, head of the ESL program for migrants and refugees for Omaha Public Schools. "Students were learning English but weren't maintaining their home language, so there was a breakdown in the family," said Mayberger. "So the parents said, 'Help us learn English.'"

School officials expanded an existing program at the Yates Community

Center, a former elementary school not far from Central. Mayberger, whose daughter and two sons had been or would be Central students and were fans of Akoy, was in charge. The program offered ESL classes for parents for three hours on weekday mornings, with five levels of proficiency. The classes were "open door," which meant adults could attend as long as they wanted or needed to. Along with expanded ESL the Yates added sewing classes, a computer lab, and early childhood classes to prepare children for school. A grant from the Sherwood Foundation funded a social worker on site.

The goal was to make parents proficient in English so that they could raise bilingual children. Early in her career Mayberger had worked for the New York City school system and had been dismayed to see second- and third-generation students in ESL classes. "What I realized is that you want to do things right as soon as families get here," Mayberger said. "If we teach them well, they should be able to raise children bilingually, and hopefully families will stay bilingual. If we do things right with the first generation, we can head off long-term societal problems."

Omaha Public Schools served about 1,350 refugee students in 2011. South Sudan and its border countries accounted for about 40 percent, while about 60 percent came from Myanmar, Bhutan, and other Southeast Asian countries. Nearly 6,800 students, or about 13 percent of the district's enrollment, were native speakers of a language other than English. Most came from rural areas of Mexico and Latin America, were not classified as refugees, and spoke Spanish as their first language.

All of Omaha's seven high schools, eleven middle schools, and sixty-two elementary schools had ESL programs with ESL-trained teachers and staff. Other supports included family-resources centers in twenty schools, dual-language classes at six schools for Spanish and English, teen literacy centers at two middle schools and district headquarters, and ESL classes for parents in targeted schools as well as at the Yates.

A teen literacy center for non-English speakers aged 13–21 operated out of the fourth floor of district headquarters. There students got intensive instruction with the goal of a third-grade proficiency in English and basic proficiency in other core subjects. This was the first school experience for some refugee and immigrant students. Because newcomers had so much to learn before they aged out of the program at twenty-one, they took no fall or spring breaks and attended a special Saturday school and two months of summer school, twice as long as mainstream students.

Apart from the school system ESL classes were offered at Metro Community College and Omaha Public Library. Adaw and Madut had attended ESL classes at the South Sudanese Community Association (which became the Refugee Empowerment Center) before they had applied for their drivers' licenses. Adaw's proficiency increased to where she could pass the naturalization test, while Madut's did not.

Mayberger's connection to her ESL program ran deep in her Nebraska blood. Her great-grandparents were Czech immigrants whose rural Nebraska experience mirrored that of the Shimerda family in Willa Cather's century-old novel *My Antonia*. "They spoke Czech as a first language, and their children spoke Czech," Mayberger said. "My mother's first language was Czech, even though she was third or fourth generation because a lot of her community spoke Czech."

Mayberger's mother, whose maiden name was Voboril, grew up in the farming community of David City, Nebraska. Her mother's family was able to farm throughout the twentieth century without English as its first language, just as Akoy's father worked at meat-processing plants with limited English. But proficiency is needed today, Mayberger said, for most jobs and economic opportunity. That's the carrot her ESL program holds out to refugee and migrant parents. "I just feel language is power," Mayberger said. "If you can help a parent learn English, how could they not be better able to parent in the U.S.?"

As Somali Bantu refugees protested in Omaha, Arab Spring swept over the Middle East and North Africa. A populist movement against autocratic rule, it began in Tunisia and spread to civil uprisings in Egypt and Bahrain; street demonstrations in Algeria, Iraq, Jordan, Kuwait, Morocco, and Oman; and insurgencies in Syria, Libya, and Yemen. Social media fueled the insurrections with messages and images of discontent—and organized protests—on Twitter, Facebook, and YouTube.

Arab Spring was born of idealism and hope for democratic reform, but instead it caused the largest upsurge of refugees since World War II. On World Refugee Day in June 2011 UN secretary general Ban Ki-moon cited the "unfolding crisis in North Africa and the Middle East" for bringing the worldwide population of forcibly displaced persons up to almost 44 million. He called on the United States, Canada, Europe, and Australia to provide more help:

> Poor countries host vastly more displaced people than wealthier ones. While anti-refugee sentiment is heard loudest in industrialized countries, developing nations host 80 per cent of the world's refugees. This situation demands an equitable solution. No one wants to become a refugee. No one should have to endure this humiliating and arduous ordeal. Yet, millions do. Even one refugee forced to flee, one refugee forced to return to danger is one too many. On this year's World Refugee Day, I ask people everywhere to spare a thought for the millions of children, women and men who have been forced from their homes, who are at risk of their lives, and who, in most cases, want nothing more than to return home or to start afresh. Let us never lose sight of our shared humanity.

Legislation proposed in the U.S. Senate and House, called the Refugee Protection Act, sought to protect refugees and asylum seekers from a rising tide of fear and xenophobia. Middle Eastern refugees in particular faced suspicion of terrorist intent. Senate sponsor Patrick Leahy, a Vermont Democrat, said, "The bill ensures that innocent asylum seekers and refugees are not unfairly denied protection as a result of overly broad terrorism bars that can have the effect of sweeping in those who were actually victimized by terrorists. The bill ensures that those with actual ties to terrorist activities will continue to be denied entry to the United States."

Sudan sidestepped Arab Spring because in January 2011 it allowed South Sudan to vote for independence. By then the strife that had started in the late 1950s had cost the lives of two million and displaced another four million in South Sudan. More than 3.8 million votes were cast by the South Sudanese and by expatriates in eight countries. Polling booths were opened in Nebraska and seven other states, and voting was conducted in an atmosphere "electric with excitement," according to a refugee service provider in Omaha. Adaw and Madut voted to secede from the Khartoum government and explained their votes to their children. "We told them Sudan has a war, and war is what brought us here," Adaw recalled. "We explain that north and south need to separate and that we pray for peace. Then we tell them they need to focus on America. They have a good life here; they go to good schools. We tell them to make their future in America."

Results were announced in February; more than 98 percent had voted to secede. Of the 8,487 South Sudanese who cast their ballots in the United States, Omaha accounted for about 36 percent of the votes. Of 3,076 votes cast in Omaha, 3,054 were for secession. The formal inauguration of South Sudan was set for July. It was born rich, with half of the former Sudan's oil wealth. But its challenges, as outlined by a congressional report, began with its need as a land-locked state to take its oil to market through pipelines and ports in Sudan. Economic development was hamstrung by minimal infrastructure—roads, airports, telephone and electric services— and by a shortage of skilled labor. Of its population of 10.5 million, 72 percent were under thirty, adult literacy was 27 percent, and more than 51 percent lived below the poverty line. An estimated 38 percent had to walk more than thirty minutes to collect drinking water. Climate change and decreased rainfall threatened agriculture, which employed about 80 percent of the population.

The hope was that an independent South Sudan would bring about peace, stability, economic development, an end to the refugee diaspora, and repatriation for those who had left. Adaw and Madut prayed that her mother and his brother in South Sudan would be safe at long last.

Meanwhile, Akoy bonded with Central's first-year principal, Dr. Keith Bigsby, whose resume included a stint as a basketball coach. They stood side by side in the hallways, Central's odd power couple. Akoy hung with Bigsby because, well, a guy never knew when a principal would come in handy. Bigsby hung with Akoy because he genuinely liked him and because it raised his "cool" factor with the student body.

Then, too, Bigsby understood Akoy's value to Central's brand, which he feared was at risk. The state had slapped it with a "persistently lowest achieving school" (PLAS) designation because its graduation rate had averaged 74.2 percent from the years 2007–2010, a shade below the 75 percent crossbar set by the state. The designation was more of a bureaucratic technicality than evidence of academic malaise, but Bigsby worried that it undercut the school's image. He worried about a lot of things: that charter school proponents were out to get Central, that white middle-class kids from the western suburbs would stay away and thus "tip" the school's delicate socioeconomic balance, and that barbarians—that is, street gangs—were at Central's gate.

Bigsby also worried about student behavior, which he believed had spun out of control in recent years. In his first month on the job he gave a talk in the auditorium that was disrupted by an unruly student. Bigsby banished the student to his office, and the next morning Bigsby had the offender make an apology to the entire school over the intercom system. It wasn't long before Bigsby drafted Akoy as an enforcer.

"We had a problem on the first floor after lunch when kids came down from the cafeteria," Bigsby recalled. "Some kids didn't understand expectations, and some were basketball players. Akoy would come and stand with me. And if somebody got out of hand and Akoy called him out, that was the end of it. In a sense, he became official. He took on a huge role."

Bigsby practiced the "seven correlates" of successful schools and promoted the "Eagle Way," which encompassed lofty attributes of scholarship and citizenship. To lighten the mood he kept up a running gag about pop star Justin Bieber in his morning intercom announcement. To the broader community he proclaimed Central "Champ High" and "the best downtown high school in the country." Bigsby knew that good PR required a team effort: administrators, faculty, and alumni. Within a year Susie Buffett's

Sherwood Foundation would start the nonprofit Nebraska Loves Public Schools to resist the onslaught of charters. Even students could help with PR, Bigsby realized—particularly naturalized refugees who were personable and poised and delivered state basketball championships as dependably as spring brought young love.

Going forward, Akoy would be the unofficial face of Central, the de facto "ambassador." When possible, he would greet officials, VIPs, and alumni. When eighth graders came for Open House, he would lead them through the old wooden hallways so that when it came time to pick a high school, they were star-struck: "Mom, guess who I met at Central today?"

Akoy began to wrap his mind around the notion that he was a role model. A letter came in the mail from a boy in the middle of the state. Central had played in Kearney, Nebraska (population thirty-two thousand) in February. He read the letter to a teacher, Michelle Synowiecki.

"Thanks for coming to our town," Akoy read. "I loved watching you play. Good luck in the future." A smile lit up his face.

"Somebody looks up to me," he said.

"You know what to do," Synowiecki replied.

"Write him back?"

"Yes."

@ZerotheHeroAkoy   **10**

As a new citizen Akoy did what red-blooded American youth did in 2011:
he started a Twitter account. After its debut in 2006 with one thousand
users, Twitter had eighteen million users by the end of 2009, among them
mogul and reality TV host Donald Trump. Arab Spring catapulted Twitter
to one hundred million active users by the middle of 2011. No slouch on
Facebook, Akoy wasn't about to fall behind on social media. He agonized
over a Twitter handle that would do justice to his persona. Then he remembered a phrase a female admirer had printed on a sign and brought to a
basketball game and subsequently had posted in a photo on Facebook. "It
said 'Akoy, Zero the Hero,'" he recalled. "I took it from there."

Akoy wore number zero, which rhymed with hero. @ZerotheHeroAkoy
was born, with ego aloft and tongue in cheek. "Some people thought it was
catchy; a few thought it was cocky," he recalled.

Akoy's debut on Twitter came as high-profile athletes embraced it to
connect with fans, dispense opinions, and shill for products and services.
Within a year Akoy's role model, LeBron James, would have 4.2 million
followers and rank fourth among pro athletes, behind soccer stars Kaká and
Cristiano Ronaldo and retired NBA legend Shaquille O'Neal. Hashtags such
as Tim Tebow's #tebowing and Jeremy Lin's #SiLinsanity would become
cultural touchstones.

Twitter's appeal—and pitfall—was that it was unfiltered and immediate.
Pittsburgh Steelers running back Rashard Mendenhall tweeted his doubts
about the events of 9/11 and sympathized with Osama bin Laden, after
which Champion canceled his endorsement deal. Kansas City Chiefs running back Larry Johnson tweeted an insult about his coach, then tweeted
a gay slur at a fan, and then was released.

"Social Networking: Gift or Curse?" was the headline of a *Central High Register* article in April 2011. Student reporter Shaleigh Karnik wrote, "If it goes on the internet it will stay there forever. Some don't realize that before they express some feelings and say things they would never say out loud. . . . Saying what is on your mind can lead to the possibility of not getting a job or not getting into the college you want."

Within a year the *Register* would run an editorial critical of the Twitter account @CentralProbs, which served as a dustbin for anonymous snark about the school:

> Although the account was perhaps originally created to get a boom in followers and start a few laughs, much of the content is arguably malicious, crude and could be misinterpreted as a form of cyber-bullying. "Ghetto" could be easily slapped onto a few of the tweets ranging from ones discussing procrastination problems, sleeping in class and waking up with a cockroach on your legs, or the problem you face with multiple "baby mommas" in the same class. . . . Staff members referenced are tied with sexual jokes, very personal life-rumors and accusations that should not be made public. . . . The Twitter account portrays our downtown school as a ghetto, sex-filled and undereducated with illegitimate faculty members type of learning facility, a message that no school would want to be promoted.

Such was the context of Akoy's first tweet, a test run, on June 29, 2011: "Checkin out twitter." The next day his second tweet foreshadowed the barrage to come: "Saw car accident today. Brought back bad memorys! Can't sleep."

Twitter became Akoy's preferred mode of expression for a while. Over the summer he challenged himself to lay down a thousand tweets. His tweets of July and August are a virtual diary of his summer, the footprints of a hoops prodigy and film buff. As the summer wore on, his tweets evolved a new sensibility, away from faux street dialect to a tamer, mainstream prose, by turns clever, poignant, and mundane.

July 2

At macdonalds with my lovely girlfriend Jessica and her bestfriend Kori (who we trying to teach to be black)!!!!!!
White Chicks tryina pickout a brotha hair! That's siiiiiiiiicccccckkkkkkk!!!!

July 3

Chillin with my other family! Having a great time talking about parents beatin us! And how they all use to be stoned when they were young!

July 5

Staying up the whole night with my bro Tarir! Leaving for Philly in the morning! Won't be back maybe for a whole month summer basketball!!!!

July 7, Philadelphia

Met John Wall and Jason Terry all in the same day!!
Day three of Reebok breakout challenge!
Long day at camp! Played ok! Back in the room eatin! Tired like crazy!!

July 9

Last day of camp was pretty good! Great opportunity and has fun! Learned a lot of new things! Now waiting to leave for Saint Louis tomorrow!

July 10

Going to sleep! Flight leaving to Saint Louis at 7:30am! Then game at 10:30! That's crazy ima retired by the end of high school!

July 11, St. Louis

One dryer and washer at the front. . . . That's when you know your at a bad hotel!!! Lol
#whoeverimarry needs to know I'm African and I don't tolerate them doing anything besides being a housewife!! Lol

Got to much stuff going on in my life!!!!!!!!!!!

July 13, Minneapolis

Mall of America was fun! Back in the hotel chillin bout to go to bed!
Two games tnwrw here in minneapolish!!!
Time to prove I'm the best there is in the game! Going to win this
tournament!!

July 15, Omaha

Finally home! Happier then ever!!! Missed my bed and everything!!
Bball takes me away from church, without the Lord I wouldn't be
who I am today! Time to go and pray!
Just got back from church, so happy I went!!!

July 18

So many choices. What to do. . . . .
Man I don't feel like cleaning this messing room! Shouldve never let
it get this bad! Dangit!!!!
Feel like hoopin! Might just go do that!!
3 people kicked out of my house! That's crazy!!!!!
Just found out we start school in exactly a month! #crazy

July 21, St. Louis

Just got to Saint Louis 8 hour drive #longride
@lilone_haha see when your African you don't have to worry about
getting sunburnt!!! Lmao!
Boring as hell! Ain't nothing to do in Saint Louis! Ready to play but
don't play until later tonight! #timegoingtoslow
Won first game! Tired as hell! Going to bed! Goodnight!

July 24

@KodyGilbow @kingjames Lebron weak he my favorite player but
he need to hurry take over the heat win his championships and
be the greatest!

I need more followers!!!

Tell me why I am up watching this new cartoon called Thunder Cats! Lmao! Can't fall asleep for some reason!

Just got our asses kicked!!!! Heading home tmwrw!!!

July 25

About to leave Saint Louis and head back to Nebraska the good life! 8 hour drive, damn long as hell! Super tired! Might sleep the whole way!

July 26, Omaha

Just got home! Damn home sweet home! Been gone too long! Ready to lay on my own bed!!

Man I'm going overseas to play basketball, skipping college!!

So bored!!!

July 27

@African_King_ mom trippin! I haven't really been home!!!

Just got asked where I wanna go to college?! I'm not even a junior in high school how the heck would I know!!!

I need to go see Captain America!!

Yeah, Ima make a Captain Africa!!!

@s1McGary about too! Focusing on 2012 class now! But new offers from oregan, drake, western Kentucky, and Tennesse!

Tyrone is too damn hyper! Keeping me up from sleeping in my own damn house! #NotCool

"Ain't nothing wrong with being dark!!!

Damn we start school in like less then 2 weeks! That's crazy!!!

Ready to leave for Kansas City tmwrw morning! Let's go! Bout to win this tournament!!!!

"House chores what a dragg!!!!

I'm rich as s white man come to you show and kill yo hypeman! I'm rollinn #lilweezy finally 300 tweets! #proud

Watching Resident evil: Afterlife!

Watching the 1987 NBA finals against Lakers and Celtics! Kareem, Kevin mchale, Larry bird alm them playing!

Larry Bird just had this sick block! He cold!!!

This dude Pat Riley been around the game for a minute!!

I need a hook shot like Kareem!!! I'll be cold!!!

Magic Johnson!!!!

@trelens2012 I'm serious man! I dont see no damn African superheroes in any movies!!! In movies in general!

Watching Blade 2

Dude dying in blade remind me of fruit gushers!!

July 28, Kansas City

In Kansas City won first game, almost lost too, to a bunch of 15s!

Need to shower! Hate to get in to shower, but when I do get in I don't want to get out!!! #weird

Just got back from grocery shopping! Got a lot of food! #smash

Watching Troy! Black people don't watch Troy! Lol

@trelens2012 gunna make TOO much money!!!

@Bongweezy24 @african_king_ dude I remember when YOU, George, victor and Ty, and augustino use to beat me up! Now I'm a beat!!!

My #CaptainAfrica movie bout to be sick!!!!!

I need to get more people for my movie tho!

@Bongweezy24 @african_king_ nobody can mess with me anymore!!

@African_King_ @bongweezy24 he is a midget and still is! It's like impossible to fight a fast midget!!!

July 29

Just found out Kansas, North Carolina and a bunch of other schools coming to our game! Going to sleep now!!! Night! #excited

Got to get up early and go watch boring NCAA video!! #lame

Just went and had the NCAA talk and stuff bout all the rules!!!

Too hungry thank God we got my favorite cereal #Cinnamontoast-crunch

Eating cereal, watching Tom and Jerry, and listening to music!

Wanna go to sleep but got a game in an hour!!

Time to go! #gametime

Need to win!

Game earlier were down by 22 came back and won! I hit game winning layup with 2.9 seconds left in overtime! #intense

July 30

Won both games today! One game tmwrw either play at 3 or 7! Semis win then off to the championship on Sunday!!

Semifinals game: SYF vs Team Nebraska Express at 3:15!! #letsgetit

Beat SYF today buy 17. Championship game tomorrow at 10:15 vs the Saint Louis Eagles! Going to be a great game!

July 31

Watching GangLand this is #crazy

Eating that Live cereal #Cinnamontoastcrunch

Championship Saint Louis Eagles Vs Team Nebraska Express #GameTime

Lost to the Saint Louis eagles in the championship by 8! #shouldvewon

Oh well! Now it's time to come back and improve

1–4 record this summer in championship games, need to improve! Gunna win everything next year!

Have so much to work on!!!!

Super tired and start school in two weeks! #wtf

I need to sleep for a month!!!!

I hope I picked up some more offers this summer!

Summer aau basketball is officially over! Had an okay summer, couldve been better!

Watching One Tree Hill

August 1, Omaha

For some reason I'm watching What I Like About You. . . . . Wow

August 2

About to go to see a movie

Cowboys & Aliens was a tight movie!

August 5

Went to take license test and on the computer it didn't say I was a citizen yet so I needed my paper! #thiswhatigetfornotbeingamerican lol

August 6

Dad finally home! Surprised he ain't get kicked out again! #nonsense

August 8

the baby hits his head on the table cries for 2 secs then goes right back! got a bruise by his eye badass

havent tweeted in a while lost my dang ipod #missit

August 9

Watching beauty and the beast! #oldmovies

End of the movie #BeautyandtheBeast where the beast becomes human! It's so cute! Lol

@Bongweezy24 lmao you stupid! You don't become soft because of a movie! #idiot

@FreakALeekk how old do you have to be to drink wine?!

Man school coming up! I swear I probably wouldn't go to school if it wasn't for #basketball

August 10

Working

Just took the longest to put together a shelf for my bosses daughter! #messeduptoomuch

Trying to play the piano! #foundanewtalent

What can I NOT do?!?!

Think I'm going to Red Robbins with boss and daughter #bouttos-mash #starving

My job is pretty fun! #bestjobever

Listening to Lotte play the flute

The flute would be too hard to learn how to play!

use to play the viola in elementary school! #beast

Finally at 800 tweets! 1000 looks closer and closer

@TheyKnowSean oh aite! We should tell behrens to let us have a open gym up at central!

August 11

A 1000 tweets ain't gunna come easy before school starts on Tuesday! #faster

Working longer then I thought! Oh well!

I'm that star up in the sky #theworldsgreatest

August 12

@D_OTTO24 at this office for like pregnant people! For my friends mom! Shes a doctor!

Got to get use to getting up early in the morning! School here in 3 days! #siiiiiiiccccccckkkk

Early morning breakfast! #IHOP! Come hungry, leave happy! Lol

I swear people dont know how to drive these days!

I wish I had a twin! #siiiiiiiccccccckkkk

Dropping basketball and taking a rapping career! #letsgooooo

The rap game is easy I'm fly like chris breezy! #letsgooooo

New Drake song Headlines is #siiiiiiiccccccckkkk

What goes around comes back around! #Beyonce

Yeah I hate contacts! Take way to damn long!!! #frustrating

I make the young girls squeal!

August 13

Just saw the cutest little girl ever at target, she sounded like a little
   chipmunk #cantwaittohavekids

Don't worry guys I'm going to wait

Tweeting till my fingers fall off!!

2 more days till nine months of hell #school

I'm fat #needtolooseweight bout to go on #biggestloser

How do you judge a tree?!?!?

August 14

Went to 2 church services this morning! #supertired

My mom is crazy!!!

This dude spongebob can't sing! #nottalented

This dude maguy starts school tomorrow! Lmao! This bout to be
   funny!

August 15

Watching American Pie #funny

Watching A Nightmare on Elm Street

Took my brother to school first day of high school for him! #goodluck

I remember my first day of high school #supernervous didn't even
   sleep! Lol

Man after two years I still don't know my way around central #ter-
   riblememory lo

Working! Scanning papers!

I don't like reading the news paper unless I'm on it! #justsaying

Ann Sjulin just thinks she #knows #everything!

Mrs. Sjulin just said she needs tape! Ima tweet everything she says!

How did this hapen Why did I let it hapen, It happened so fast culdnt
   control myself! It's kinda good but not really! Dnt want to hurt any 1

1000 tweets!! #finallymadeit

Families

Home life was tense. Adaw and Madut struggled in their marriage.

"It was a time when my parents were up and down, arguing, fighting at the house," Akoy recalled. "They couldn't be in the same place without something brewing up between them. I didn't try to get involved too much. Every once in a while the argument got out of hand. If the kids were around, I would try to take them outside. I would tell my parents to calm it down or argue later when the kids weren't around. I did what I could to help.

"My mom didn't always work. With the babies she wasn't always able to work. So it was my dad working and having to pay all the bills and my mom getting on him for those things. If we needed something, my dad would say, 'We can't really do this and also pay the bills; you need to get a job.' My mom was trying to go to school and take ESL courses, and my dad says, 'We're struggling to pay the bills, and you want to go to school and get backpacks for the kids.'"

Marital stress came with the African refugee experience, an outgrowth of financial struggle, absence of extended family, and disruption of traditional gender roles. African wives asserted themselves as co-equals in the United States in ways they could not in their native lands. "The men resent some of these rights, and deem it unacceptable," wrote Amadu Swaray, a divorce attorney in Minnesota and native of Sierra Leone whose clients were African. "They see them as challenges to their masculinity. In most cases, their reactions lead to frictions, which in turn, cause marital problems, and many of the marital problems lead to divorce."

Adaw pleaded with Akoy to help with household expenses. He took his problem to Lotte, who relayed it to her mother. Ann was an obstetrician/gynecologist in a private practice. Her group occupied a building with a vacant first floor to be cleaned and a yard to be weeded. She offered the work to Akoy at ten dollars an hour.

"It won't be easy," Ann said. "Are you sure you want it?"

"I'm sure."

Akoy worked two or three days a week throughout the last month of the summer, around his basketball schedule. Some of the work was in Ann's office, scanning and filing. Sometimes Lotte dropped by, and sometimes Akoy joined Lotte and Ann for dinner. Akoy and Lotte drew closer, even as Akoy continued to see Jessica. A tweet from August 15, 2011, spoke to Akoy's dilemma: "How did this hapen Why did I let it hapen, It happened so fast culdnt control myself! It's kinda good but not really! Dnt want to hurt any 1"

Akoy's junior year at Central began with a warning from his counselor, Bette Ball: his grades needed to come up to qualify for a D-1 scholarship. He took it to heart and started a before-school math tutorial, with the help of assistant athletic director Paul Nielson. He also asked for help from Ann, who agreed to hire him a math tutor. "But you have to do it at our house because I can't get a math tutor to you," Ann said.

Akoy found rides to Ann's office at Seventy-Second and West Center Road at the end of her work day and rode home with her. He got tutored in math, ate dinner with the Sjulins, and stayed through the evening. Lotte, an accomplished student, helped Akoy in his other courses. He came to appreciate the Sjulins' home for its well-stocked refrigerator, spaciousness, quiet, and dependable internet, in contrast to his own quarters, cramped with guest uncles and loud with rambunctious siblings. Sometimes he brought his laundry.

"Is Akoy loving Lotte, or is it that you're taking care of him?" Dave asked his wife. "I hope he likes Lotte," Ann said.

When Akoy stayed late, Ann drove him home, thirty minutes in each direction, but some nights he stayed at the Hammers', who were closer by in west Omaha. Ann knew that relatives, friends, and colleagues were curious about Akoy's presence and that the unspoken subtext was race. Her acceptance, she knew, came from the context of her own upbringing and faith. She was a fourth-generation Nebraskan from Sutherland, which had a mostly white population of 840, a Union Pacific train yard, and a few grain silos. Her father and mother had married after they met at the upper crust Ak-Sar-Ben Ball in Omaha. Then her father had gone into the grain business with his father-in-law. "My parents were always inclusive," Ann said. "When we went places, if my mom saw someone by themselves, she would invite them to talk with us. My dad was friendly to everybody. They never thought anybody was too poor or too rich or too anything. They treated everybody the same."

Sutherland had one ten-room motel, Ann recalled, that would fill to capacity when winter storms hit and I-80 was shut down. The motel asked Ann's parents and other local residents to shelter stranded motorists. "We had a four-bedroom house, and my dad always said, 'Yes, who do you have?'" she recalled. "We'd put people on our couch and in our bedrooms. That happened several times."

Ann's father once met a young man from Sweden over breakfast at a gas station, Ann recalled. The youth was on his way to school in California. A week later her father got a call from the youth in California; he had been denied admission and needed a job. "He came and lived with us for six weeks and painted our house," Ann recalled. "I'm a seventeen-year-old girl in high school, and my dad never worried that a twenty-year-old boy was in the house with his daughter. My dad never knew a stranger. He would let anybody live in his house."

Ann attended the University of Nebraska–Lincoln and went on to medical school at the University of Nebraska Medical Center in Omaha. There she met Dave, who had grown up in Shenandoah, Iowa, where his family had a nursery business. They married in 1987, got their medical degrees in 1989, and served residencies in Omaha. Ann went on to build her career with Mid-City Ob-Gyn, where one of her patients was Leisha Hammer, whose son Trae she delivered. (When Leisha Hammer found out Akoy worked in Ann's office, she warned him, "Stay out of my file.")

Dave specialized in ear, nose, and throat and eventually landed at the Boys Town Ear Nose and Throat Institute on the campus made iconic by the 1938 film that starred Spencer Tracy as Father Edward Flanagan, founder of the orphanage. Boys Town was a symbol of compassion and charity, save for an episode of financial corruption in the early 1970s. "I really feel that the spirit of Father Flanagan is in everything we do," Dave said in promotional video for the institute.

The Sjulins were committed to their Lutheran faith and did their best to pass it on to their three daughters. "God has blessed us in a huge way, and it's our job to be a blessing to others," Ann said. "It's what Jesus would do." The inclusiveness of Ann's childhood and of Dave's workplace informed the sensibilities of their daughters. "My kids have a lot of heart for people in other cultures," Ann said. "Lotte always was drawn to kids who are multiracial. I remember one of her teachers adopted Chinese kids, and she wanted to be with them. We laughed and said, 'What is the deal?' and she said, 'Oh, they're so cute.'"

Lotte had not had a boyfriend before she met Akoy. Right off, she liked his "silly" sense of humor. She was an athlete, dedicated to fitness, and admired his athleticism. She came to appreciate his personality in full. "He could be super outgoing and super reserved; he found a balance" Lotte recalled. "He was personable. He knew how to talk to everybody, and everybody seemed to love him. It was fun to be around him, and he was cool to be in public with. People know who you are when you're 6–8 and have all those championships. Anybody could strike a conversation with him.

"He always did something special, even if it seemed like he wasn't listening. He recalled a lot of small details. I could tell he put a lot of thought into his day-to-day actions and how he treated people. He understood things differently than other people I had met, which I liked. He was an independent thinker—he relied on himself."

Ann watched Lotte and Akoy's deepening attraction with bewilderment. Sometimes Akoy arrived at their house after he had been out with Jessica. Ann thought the situation was "weird" until one evening Lotte told her that Akoy had asked her to Central's homecoming dance.

"What happened to his girlfriend?" Ann asked.

"I guess she's not the girlfriend anymore."

Akoy wrote of his life as a junior with candor and humor. He was angry Adaw left her car with an empty gas tank more than once and expected him to fill it up now that he had a paycheck. "Should've never did it the first time!!" he wrote. But his admiration for Adaw was undeniable after she broke up a scrum between him and one of his brothers: "Wow! My mom stronger than me!!" Annoyed with an unidentified female, he borrowed from a song he had heard: "So you make love to me on Saturday and confess on Sunday?!?! Lmao #SMDH."

Akoy's humor could be ribald, as when he wrote of his teammate Tra-Deon Hollins, who had a girlfriend: "Tre just said who uses condoms these days? He ain't lying!" Somebody did because he subsequently wrote, "My bro just went to the nurse and asked for a #condom." For those who did not, but should have, he cracked, "Kids in the back seat cause accidents, and accidents in the back seat cause kids! #SMDH so true." His humor could be irreverent, as in his reaction to the death of Apple CEO Steve Jobs: "[This] screws up my plans of getting the I-Phone 5 #DANGIT." And he could poke fun at himself, noting that he danced awkwardly: "Being 6'9 and my knees trying to dance DO NOT GO TOGETHOR!!!!!!!"

When the first hint of cold came in mid-September, Akoy fell back on a stock gag: "This is when I wish I was still in Africa!" As temperatures dropped in October, he wrote, "It's that time of the season when Africans don't come outside and school absences go up. Cause they probably at home with that heat high as possible and cuddled under 6 blankets. Lol." He skipped a Friday night football game "cause Africans and cold weather don't mix." He struggled with Nebraska's frigid winters. "What was the first Sudanese person thinking when he came to Nebraska?" Akoy wondered aloud. "Going from 110 degrees to a place that gets below zero. It makes no sense to me."

He took on his studies with a new determination that rendered them no more palatable. Of his Spanish class he wrote, "I already speak three languages!! I don't have room in my brain to learn another language!!" Honors physics was a nightmare, and history demanded too much reading, though it provoked him to observe, "Learning about the Aztecs!! These fools were brutal. No regard for human life!!!"

The problem with school, Akoy decided, was that too much of it was irrelevant to everyday life. "I won't need any of this unless we go into these fields," he wrote. The writings of old English authors fell into his irrelevant category, as did statistics, pre-calculus, and biology. He wanted practical education that would help him apply for a mortgage, invest, raise children, or design a website. Government, history, and a business course taught by Colleen Lenners he deemed useful and relevant. Even as he groused, his grades improved dramatically, which delighted him. "I ask myself how I've gotten to care so much about school and getting good grades. . . . I'm even staying up this late doing homework," he wrote. He answered his own rhetorical question: "Charlotte and the Sjulin family! thank you!"

On November 28, his birthday, Akoy wrote, "Man I feel old as hell turning 17 today! #oldmaniam." But basketball season was just around the corner, and he could barely wait for it to start.

Prior to the season Akoy wrote, "The game of basketball brings great #joy to me!" Years later, when I asked him to describe his joy in basketball, Akoy said it gave him a sense of urgency, an outlet for his emotions, and a bond with his teammates. "In the end," he said, "it's just fun."

Perfection   **12**

Akoy's prophecy gained inspiration before his junior season. For the first time he learned, from Behrens, that he could make Nebraska history. Nobody ever had played on four straight boys Class A state championship basketball teams in Nebraska. Lincoln Northeast (1995–98) had won four straight in Class A, but no individual had played on all four. Jason Glock had played on Wahoo's four-peat (1988–91) and Kelly Prater had played on Clearwater's (1984–87). Falls City Sacred Heart (1988–91) had won four straight with Steve Simon a starter on all four, and Adam Froeschl, Kent Knobbe, and Jeff Schawang members of all four teams. Glock, Prater, and Simon were stars, but Wahoo was in Class B and Clearwater and Sacred Heart were in Class D, for smaller schools. Class A was the iron in Nebraska.

Energized by his newfound knowledge, in September 2011 Akoy wrote, "If I win state for the next 2 years I might be the only Class A player to ever win 4 state titles in a row! #lookatmenow."

Indeed wherever Akoy went, people looked at all 6 feet, 8 inches of him. Yet even as he chased a record that by definition could not be broken, he began to worry about something that could: his body. He had been in two car accidents and taken hits in football as a sophomore. He had ridden long hours to grassroots basketball destinations across the Midwest. School desks and seats at public venues were too small. His diet as a young boy in Sudan and Egypt had lacked nutrients. The cumulative effect was a sore back that seemed more chronic than not. As the season got underway he wrote the following:

Yeah cant feel my back! #notagoodtobehurt.

Man why i always got to be hurt during basketball season?? can never
be healthy!!!

Im gunna have a short career!!

He sought treatment in late December and wrote, "At the chiropractor for my back! lord i hope they can fix it!!" In late January he wrote of
more treatment: "Chiropractor appointment! #bodyproblems." By then
his frustration spilled into his writing: "Injuries Injuries Injuries why i
have so many of them!"

Akoy's ailments were generally unknown to the public, which saw him
as the durable engine of a juggernaut. Central was the preseason favorite of most of the coaches and savants in Nebraska. Expectations were
so high that the *Omaha World-Herald* speculated that the Eagles might
"run the table" for a perfect season, a feat last accomplished in 1988–89
by Millard South.

Though Akoy was the celebrity face of the team, he had plenty of support on a squad as deep as any Behrens had coached. Most notable was
Tra-Deon Hollins, a junior 6-foot-2 guard and defensive prodigy whose
training as a boxer gave him lightning-fast hands. Hollins had become
a starter midway through his sophomore season and had nursed a few
perceived slights. He thought he should have played varsity as a freshman, though Behrens had thought otherwise, and he believed his rep as
a "defensive specialist" disrespected his offensive ability. He chafed in the
shadow cast by Akoy.

"Tra-Deon had a chip on his shoulder about the attention Akoy got,"
Behrens recalled. "He thought he was as good and as valuable, and he was
probably right. They didn't always get along at practice. They would go at
it. Tra-Deon was an ultra-competitive type of kid."

Now Hollins emerged as a team leader alongside Akoy. One teammate
saw their leadership as a "good cop–bad cop" combination. "Tra-Deon
was the bad cop," recalled Tre'Shawn Thurman, then a sophomore forward. "He would get on you: 'C'mon man, do your job.' Then Akoy would
come over and put his arm around your shoulder: 'It's all right man; we

gonna get it right." Akoy had the knowledge of winning. Tra-Deon had the heart and hustle."

Hollins's immersion in basketball was made more complete by his girlfriend, Paige Muhammad, who started for Central's girls varsity, which would go on to win state in early March. Two other starters were back from the 2011 championship: senior guard Darian Barrientos-Jackson and junior guard Deandre Hollins-Johnson. The fifth starter was the 6-foot-6 Thurman, another Scott Hammer protégé projected by Behrens as a future star. Thurman's bloodlines traced to the defunct Tech High, where his great-uncles Larry, Ernie, and Kim Britt were standout athletes. Ernie Britt had played football and basketball alongside future Heisman Trophy winner Johnny Rodgers in the late 1960s. Senior forward Deshun Roberts, senior guard Mike Welch, and junior guard K. J. Scott, a prized transfer from Benson High and a cousin to Hollins and Hollins-Johnson, rounded out what became an eight-man rotation. Scott played grassroots ball for Hammer, and his transfer had further incited rival high school coaches against Hammer.

The season tipped off in early December, and Central won three games by wide margins to capture the Jamboree Tournament. In mid-December the Eagles ran their record to 6-0 as Akoy shot 80 percent and scored 21 points against Millard West. They rang in 2012 and won the Holiday Tournament with a 61–46 victory over South to improve to 11-0. At that point their smallest victory margin was 15 points. A buzz saw of a press was their trademark. "We trapped the whole game," Thurman recalled. "Me and Tra-Deon were the first trap. I was on the ball; he guarded the guy who got the ball. We ran the full length every possession. Akoy was lucky—he got to sit back. If they broke the press, he blocked the shot. If they scored, I took the ball out and got it to Tra-Deon. Other teams might press a little and go back to half court, but we pressed the whole game. We had the depth; we could sub in three or four guys and keep it up. We had the conditioning—Behrens made sure of that. We had the speed, the depth, the conditioning, and talent to press the whole game."

Akoy's defense was an insurance policy. Behrens estimated that he blocked or altered 10–12 shots a game. A blocked shot was not enough for Akoy; the block had to be controlled. "When you block them out of bounds, everybody can 'ooh' and 'aah' but they get the ball back," Akoy told a reporter. "If I block to myself or a teammate, it provides us more possessions. I've learned to block softly to me or, if I see a teammate, I'll block it to them. It all comes with chemistry, and my teammates know they have to be ready for the ball." Opponents shot at 32.5 percent, compared to 47 percent the season before Akoy arrived. The *World-Herald*'s Sam McKewon described Central as "a controlled chaos of plugged passing lanes, quick traps, blocked shots, runaway dunks and sudden bursts of points. Speed. Defense. Pressure. Teamwork."

Offense was distributed so that the top scorers, Akoy, Hollins, and Barrientos-Jackson, averaged a modest 12–13 points. Team goals prevailed, Behrens thought, because most of his players had been showcased on the summer grassroots circuit. "Nobody felt pressure to score," Behrens said. "They were unselfish because we didn't need anybody to put up huge numbers. If we kept winning, we would be on the news and social media. They realized they would get more attention than the guy on the .500 team who averages 20."

The Eagles went to 19-0 after a 63–48 win over eighth-ranked Millard North. A close first half hinted at a pitfall of dominance. "We just kind of got lazy," Akoy told a reporter. "Sometimes we can get a little complacent." Then they beat fourth-ranked South, for the third time, 82–64, to go to 20-0. Things were good in school as well, as Akoy wrote, "Guess who made the Honor Roll #AkoyAgau feeling very educated."

Against third-ranked Papillion–La Vista, Akoy was whistled for his fourth foul, after which he muttered to an official and was slapped with a technical, his fifth foul. His teammates played without him for the last twelve minutes and won anyway, 63–46, to go to 23-0. They beat Bryan by 17 and Bellevue East by 22 to get to 25-0. The state tournament was in three weeks and perfection seemed perfectly attainable, until suddenly it did not.

On Saturday, February 18, 2012, Akoy published a series of tweets:

About to go under the knife.
Torn meniscus ready to be fixed
Bye y'all! Tweet y'all when I'm out!
Now I know what it feels like to wear tights.
Tweeting substitute to fill in for Akoy while he is in surgery.
Should be wrapping up soon #thisdoesntevenhurt
Feels wierd to have a guy inside my leg #neveragain
This should take away all my pain #newagain

Thus did Akoy live-tweet his arthroscopic knee surgery at Nebraska Ortho-paedic Hospital. It is believed to be the first live-tweet by a patient in surgery in Nebraska and possibly anywhere.

After his surgery Akoy wrote the obvious: "Who knew I could be so addicted to twitter #obsession." Post-operative care seemed to suit him:

The nurse that's taking care of me is #fineeeee
Mmmmm she is finnnee
Let the drugged up tweets begin
I love morphine

Local media were on the story by the next day. Behrens said that Akoy's right knee had been "really bothering him" for a couple of weeks and that doctors had told Akoy he would be ready to play in the state tournament and possibly in the districts. Typically meniscus surgery requires six to eight weeks of rest and rehab before strenuous exercise. The notion that Akoy could play in the districts in a week and at state in two and a half weeks defied medicine and perhaps common sense. "But no, I'm not going to miss state!" he wrote. "Well hopefully not!"

Rehab began, and Akoy wrote, "I hate physical therapy." He sat out the district semifinal against 4-19 Omaha Northwest, and the expected cake-walk turned into a nail biter. At halftime he lit into his teammates. "Some of the words shouldn't be put in the paper," he told McKewon. Central pulled out its tightest game of the season, 61–51, and punctuated Akoy's value. Ten days after surgery he was on the floor for the district final against Kearney. In a limited role he scored 5 points as Central kept Kearney off the scoreboard until the second quarter on the way to a 59–36 win. The day after he wrote, "So I tried to play last night and I sprained my ankle! #badluck. I'm going straight back to my crutches!!!"

Nineteen days after surgery Akoy was at the Devaney Center in Lincoln for the state quarterfinal. "Man I'm hyped," he wrote. "I feel like we shouldn't have school during the state tournament!" Central was 27-0 and was ranked twenty-ninth nationally by MaxPreps.com and thirty-seventh by ESPN, with an average margin of victory of 25.5 points. Not only were the Eagles good, they were colorful. As McKewon wrote in the article mentioned above, the team "is full of distinct personalities. They'll gesture with Behrens on the court—or even have an animated conversation. Before tip-off, they chant and dance in a circle. Aside from Thurman—who sports Central purple Nikes—they wear a whole variety of shoe colors. A couple wear pink Hello Kitty socks."

In pursuit of a perfect record Central sought a place among Nebraska's all-time best, which included the unbeaten squads of Millard South (1989) and Omaha South (1960), as well as Central's 1975 team, which had a single loss. A national schedule might have catapulted the Eagles into an ultra-elite that included the 2003 team of St. Vincent–St. Mary (Akron) with LeBron James; the 1989 team of St. Anthony (Jersey City NJ) with Bobby Hurley; the 1983 team of Dunbar (Baltimore) with Reggie Williams, Muggsy Bogues, and Reggie Lewis; the 1993 team of Oak Hill Academy (Virginia) with Jerry Stackhouse; the 2006 team of Lawrence (Indianapolis) North with Greg Oden and Mike Conley Jr.; and the 1964 team of Power Memorial (New York City) with Lew Alcindor (later known as Kareem Abdul-Jabbar). On the other hand, a national schedule might have exposed Central as no more than a local power. But that context, and a matchup with Oak Hill, was a year off.

The Eagles' quarterfinal opponent was Omaha Bryan, a 17-9 team they had twice beaten by wide margins. This time Bryan figured out how to neutralize the Central press. Central led 32–29 at half and 41–38 after three quarters. Late in the fourth quarter Bryan's Ethan Mantalvo stole a pass and scored on a layup to cut Central's lead to 52–50. Then he stole another pass and hit two free throws to knot the score with 1:14 left. Hollins was whistled for charging with 22 seconds left. The Devaney Center held its collective breath.

(At this point, in a dramatized Hollywood version, Akoy tweets from midcourt: "Here I come to save the day! #bringiton.")

Bryan inbounded the ball under its own basket with a chance to go ahead. Instead, with Central in its press, K. J. Scott stole the ball and drove the baseline from the left side. Scott went under the basket for a reverse layup and missed. Deshun Roberts, the senior who had not scored a point, was there for the putback and a 54–52 lead with 13.5 seconds left. Bryan missed on its next possession, and Akoy sank 2 free throws to seal a 56–52 squeaker. "I know a whole lot of people wondered what we'd do with a pressure situation," Behrens told the media. "But we got the steal and we got the winning basket when it mattered."

Akoy, whose 12 points were on free throws, wrote, "Showed us that we aren't really as good as we think we are! Everyone made some bad plays! Oh well #forgive and #forget." And he added: "Just got to improve and play hard tomorrow! Big game! Take no team for #granted."

The Eagles were better in a 67–47 semifinal win over Lincoln North Star, a game so uneventful it merited not a single tweet from Akoy.

The final against Omaha South was only a bit more suspenseful. Central trailed 27–23 at the half, at which point Behrens read the riot act. Three weeks removed from knee surgery, Akoy took control. In a burst of dominance he blocked a layup, kept the ball in bounds, and passed it to a teammate atop the key. He took a return pass in the post, spun toward the lane, and put the ball in for a 33–31 lead. On South's next possession Akoy blocked another shot and triggered a fast break bucket. Senior Darian Barrientos-Jackson got hot, and Central didn't stop until it nailed down a 55–38 victory, a state title, and a perfect 30-0 season.

In the postgame locker room, captured on Jay Landstrom's video, Behrens congratulated his players. "You just set a Nebraska record. Thirty wins. So look: myself, all the coaches, the administrators, everybody involved, we could not be prouder of you guys. You did everything you set out to do. Enjoy it."

Enjoy they did, with music and dance and exuberance, Akoy at the periphery, ceding the floor to his more rhythmic teammates. He had finished with a triple double, 16 points, 13 rebounds, and 14 blocks—another monster final to embellish his Big Game aura. His totals for three state finals were 45 points, 35 rebounds, and 30 blocks. This one, three weeks after knee surgery, was a monument to his toughness.

Yet within his perfect game within a perfect season came a moment of ignominy. Central led by 13 in the fourth quarter when a South turnover put Akoy on the receiving end of a fast-break pass. With nobody in his path, he gathered in the ball, loped toward the basket, went up for a dunk—and missed! Not only did the ball clank off the rim, Akoy crashed into the basket support. The laughter was palpable on Akoy's social media:

How does someone 6'8" miss a dunk. can u say Sprite commercial.
Can those stats make up for the terrible missed dunk?
bro try to take your dunks a lot closer
At least our African dunked unlike Central's getting rim stuffed haha

Akoy took the ribbing in good humor and fired back:

Thank you! My knee gave out and I also have 2 sprained ankles!
Omaha Central Eagles 2012 #STATECHAMPS 30-0! Yeah we didn't lose!!!
Have not gotten any sleep in the past 3 days! #celebrating #STATE-CHAMPS
Had a great time with the bros!
Damn I look good on tv! Got me lookin big!
Did I forget to say that we 30-0?!?!
And if anyone wanna bag about my missed dunk, please read my stats line!

Hey everyone that is hatin I'm lending my state titles out since I got so many! So you can feel like me for once! #mantheyaintme

The missed dunk became a source of amusement even within Central. In the final meta-scene of Jay Landstrom's highlight video, Akoy's younger brother, Maguy, now a freshman at Central, is shown at a screen viewing the video.

"Wait, wait, wait, wait," Maguy says.

"Maguy, what's the matter?" Behrens asks. "Don't you like the video?"

"It's okay, but I think we forgot one thing."

That one thing—Akoy's missed dunk—was queued as the slapstick punch line. So the joke was on Akoy. But as Nebraska basketball history forever records, he got the last laugh. Perfect.

Fig. 1. Akoy Agau at the age of six. Photo courtesy of Adaw Makier.

Fig. 2. (*opposite top*) The Dinka of South Sudan were devoted to cattle, of which they were said to be "loving slaves." Photo courtesy of JennaCB123, Wikimedia Commons.

Fig. 3. (*opposite bottom*) Akoy's mother, Adaw Makier, grew up on a farm outside the town of Wau, in South Sudan, in a cone-shaped hut with a thatched roof. Photo courtesy of Fabrizio Demartis, Wikimedia Commons.

Fig. 4. (*above*) Mason School Apartments in 2016. Photo by Steve Marantz.

Fig. 5. (*opposite top*) Scott Hammer, who guided Akoy through grassroots basketball and became his co-guardian. Photo by Steve Marantz.

Fig. 6. (*opposite bottom*) Central High School, west entrance. Reprinted with permission of Omaha Central High School Foundation.

Fig. 7. (*above*) Sudanese basketball legend Manute Bol (*center*) in Omaha in 2002, with two Central students, twins Duoth Kuon (*left*) and Both Kuon (*right*). Reprinted with permission of *Omaha Central High School O-Book*.

Fig. 8. Eric Behrens, Central's varsity coach. Reprinted with permission of *Omaha World-Herald*.

Fig. 9. Nebraska Class A state champions 2010. Reprinted
with permission of *Omaha Central High School O-Book.*

Fig. 10. Central Eagles giving the "Eagle wings" signal after winning the state tour-
nament in 2011. Back row (*left to right*): assistant coach Ben Holling, head coach Eric
Behrens, assistant coach Corey Kline, assistant principal Ed Bennett, athletic director
Darin Williams, Akoy Agau, assistant coach Jay Landstrom, assistant coach Andres
"The Don" Tapia, James Jones, assistant athletic director Paul Nielson, student manager
Anna DiRucco, principal Keith Bigsby. Middle row (*left to right*): Tre'Shawn Thurman,
Cyrell Hodges, Treytice Lee, DeShun Roberts, Camron Payne, Deandre Hollins-
Johnson, student manager Aron Sanders, ball boy Roman Behrens. Front row (*left to
right*): Mike Welch, Darian Barrientos-Jackson, Eddie Vinson, Calvin McCoy, Domi-
nique McKinzie, Paulino Gomez, Tra-Deon Hollins. Photo courtesy of Jay Landstrom.

Fig. 11. Akoy Agau became a naturalized American citizen in April 2011, along with his brothers, Maguy (*far left*) and Aguir, and sister Achol. Photo courtesy of Mike Sautter.

Fig. 12. As a junior Akoy overpowered opponents in the post as Central rolled to a 30-0 record and a third straight state title. Reprinted with permission of *Omaha World-Herald.*

Fig. 13. (*above*) Akoy's signature roar capped off a perfect season in 2011–12. Reprinted with permission of *Omaha World-Herald*.

Fig. 14. (*opposite top*) Omaha Central teammate Tra-Deon Hollins had lightning-fast hands. Reprinted with permission of *Omaha World-Herald*.

Fig. 15. (*opposite bottom*) Akoy Agau as a senior. Reprinted with permission of *Omaha World-Herald*.

Fig. 16. Coach Eric Behrens and Akoy Agau. Reprinted with permission of *Omaha World-Herald.*

Fig. 17. Akoy holds aloft a souvenir net after his fourth straight state title in 2013. Reprinted with permission of *Omaha World-Herald*.

Fig. 18. Akoy Agau and teammate Deandre Hollins-Johnson celebrate their victory in the 2013 finals over Papillion–La Vista. Credit: Ted Kirk/*Lincoln Journal Star*.

Fig. 19. Akoy wearing No. 0. An ESPN scouting report described him as "raw offensively" with a decent touch, a good rebounder, and a solid shot blocker. Credit: Francis Gardler/*Lincoln Journal Star*.

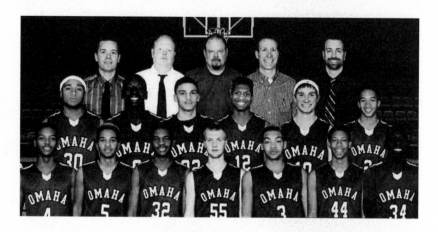

Fig. 20. (*opposite top*) The 2012–13 Central team that swept through its three games at the state tournament by a combined margin of 75 points. Reprinted with permission of *Omaha Central High School O-Book.*

Fig. 21. (*opposite bottom*) Akoy and his girlfriend, Charlotte "Lotte" Sjulin, before spring prom. Photo courtesy of Ann Sjulin.

Fig. 22. (*above*) Koang Doluony talking to a group of fifth-graders. Photo courtesy of Megan Farmer.

Fig. 23. Pulaski Park in South Omaha, a favored basketball venue for South Sudanese refugees. Reprinted with permission of *Omaha World-Herald.*

Fig. 24. Akoy holding his youngest sister, Achan, at Easter service in 2015. In front, from left, are Achol, Akol, Maguy, and Atong. Next to Akoy is Aguir. Photo courtesy of Adaw Makier.

Fig. 25. Mabel and Benjamin Marantz, circa 1956, Miami Beach. Photo courtesy of Marantz family.

Fig. 26. Akoy at graduation from Georgetown in May 2017 with his mother, Adaw, and father, Madut. Photo courtesy of Adaw Makier.

Fig. 27. Akoy playing for sMU. Photo courtesy of sMU Athletic Department.

Basketball and Business 13

With his third title in hand Akoy might well have basked in satisfaction. Instead he wrote himself into an existential funk:

Why do I happen to ruin the most dearest things that I have in my life?
I can't seem to make the best decision that fits me without people wanting to be involved!!!
Everything good in my life falling apart!!!
Change! Changes are needed in order to become a better person!!
But I'm not going to change over night!
Is it wrong to want to do something to make yourself happy?

Akoy lugged his weary body to track practice a little more than a week after the basketball final. An afternoon of high jump, triple jump, and long jump did not lighten his mood:

My body was just not made for me to be an athlete!
I'm considering #retirement.
Now I hurt my back and can barely move it!! It might be that time to really be considering it.

His disposition improved on a spring break getaway to Florida as a guest of the Sjulins. He went to Disney World, took in his first NBA game (Orlando Magic–Utah Jazz), visited the University of Florida campus with Ann, devoured ample hotel breakfasts, and soaked in the warmth. "The weather here amazes me more and more!" he wrote. "Feels like I'm back home in Africa!!" The vacation tightened the bond between Akoy and Lotte. She had become a regular presence at his home and was embraced by his siblings, though Adaw initially was circumspect. "Your grandmother save cows for you to marry a Sudanese girl," Adaw told Akoy, half in jest. As Adaw warmed to Lotte, she told Akoy his grandmother had invited the two of them to visit her in South Sudan. "She say, 'Why don't he come here with his American girl so I can bless her,'" Adaw recalled.

Back at Central Akoy took comfort in a club he had joined and come to value almost as much as basketball: the FBLA. Future Business Leaders of America was the antidote of relevance to some of his academic courses. It helped him think about the business of basketball, now upon him in an onslaught of college recruiters. Soon he would choose a college, a coach, and a basketball program, a judgment calculated much like a business plan.

FBLA was a decades-old national organization that prepared students for careers in business and information technology. Through FBLA students connected with local businesses, raised funds for local nonprofits, and explored management. Central's FBLA members sold candy bars to raise funds for the March of Dimes.

"Akoy sold a phenomenal amount of candy," recalled Denise Powers, faculty supervisor of FBLA. "I would take candy to him in the courtyard at lunchtime, and he would give me a box of money every day. It was a reason for people to meet and greet him."

Akoy also organized a dodgeball tournament that generated additional funds. Sometimes he missed part of a basketball practice to attend an FBLA meeting. He and Powers hit it off, and Akoy became a regular in her room 444, where she kept a small refrigerator stocked with 64-ounce Powerades. "Every day of the school year he came and grabbed his Powerade," said Powers. "Even when he went to state, I took his Powerade down to Lincoln and gave it to him. It was kind of a joke, but it was my way of thanking him for supporting FBLA."

FBLA members explored a business niche of their choice; for Akoy it was sports and entertainment management. He learned about network-ing, delegating, and event management, but of more interest to him was branding, marketing, and buyer behavior. In the spring FBLA students from across the state gathered at a conference that featured seminars, workshops, and competitions in their field of interest. "We competed in group activities with an opportunity to go to the nationals, but we didn't make it," recalled Powers.

The efficacy of marketing was underscored by an unexpected development that uplifted Central and surprised area educators. For the first time in its history Central had more applicants for its next freshman class than allotted seats. It capped attendance at 2,400, so 685 applicants had been accepted and more than 200 were turned away—as many as 400, according to the *Register*. Of the 685, about 485 were from affluent neighborhoods outside Central's attendance area. This surge of applicants had occurred despite the scarlet label of "persistently lowest achieving" hung around Central's neck by the state. In effect students and parents had thumbed their noses at PLAS and the stealth politics of the charter school movement. Moreover, Central had risen in stature at a time when large urban high schools elsewhere—in Chicago, Philadelphia, St. Louis, Cleveland, Kansas City—floundered. Nobody was more pleased than the principal, Bigsby, who told a reporter, "We obviously did a really good job of marketing. I'm aware of that."

Under Bigsby Central had marketed its academic excellence, its new international baccalaureate program, proximity to the downtown renaissance, a diverse student body, a safe and secure building, and (perhaps most effectively) excellence in sports. Both girls and boys teams were state champions in basketball, and the boys had won six of the last seven. Akoy was the most visible athlete in the city, and as Bigsby explained to me, his persona fed a word-of-mouth buzz that drove Central's enrollment "What he represented—and I'll never forget a parent telling me this—was a post-racial era," Bigsby recalled. "The way he presented himself, in the classroom and on the court helped kids transcend the racial divide. He had this unusual ability to cross lines. Our old white alumni fell in love with him, and African American church-going women fell in love with him. When people asked me what was great about Central, this kid was exactly the image we wanted to be. A tall, photogenic, articulate African American male respected and loved by everybody. He was our ambassador."

Akoy was modest about his contribution. "The most requested school kids want to go to! #proud," he wrote. "About us being good in education and sports! #wedeep." He was more focused on his future. Throughout the spring and summer of 2012 he was recruited by at least forty NCAA D-1 colleges. His ESPN scouting report described a player with limitations and potential:

Strengths:
Akoy is raw offensively. He scores mostly on putbacks, dump offs and tip ins inside. He is much more of a power forward right now and probably projects to that position down the road. He has a decent touch and hit a couple of shots from 19 feet. Akoy is a good rebounder. He has solid length and showed nice effort inside. His length allows him to be a solid shotblocker on defense.

Weaknesses:
He can hit some face up jump shots but that is not his strength. He can score in the low block but currently must turn and face in order to score in the paint. He has to continue to develop but he has a chance to be a good D-1 prospect down the road.

Bottom Line:
Agau, a native of Sudan, is a long, developing forward prospect with a very high ceiling. He's still raw and inexperienced, but shows flashes of becoming a dominant force in time, particularly on the defensive end.

Coaches came to meet him at Central, and they scouted him at grassroots tournaments or camps where he showcased himself. His schedule took him from Little Rock in late April to San Francisco in late May to Los Angeles in early June. Upon his return he wrote about a stressful moment at home.

My mom came in at 8:30 happy for no reason!!! Woke me up!!
Talkin bout you need to stop talking to all these college coaches cause
    I'm tired of talking to them (she has spoken to 5 coaches) lol
Not even close to the 40 or more coaches I have spoken to!!

Then she gunna tell me she quit her job working at Creighton so I could go there . . . does that make sense?!?! lol

Akoy went to Lincoln to visit with Nebraska's new coach, Tim Miles, before he was off to Charlottesville, Virginia, for a "Top 100" camp sponsored by the NBA Players Association. He showed well in Charlottesville, both on and off the court, as ESPN analyst Tim McCormick tweeted: "Akoy Agau understands the power of branding. Great handshake & eye contact when speaking . . . superb around the rim. After the camp concluded, Akoy visited the West Virginia and Georgetown campuses.

By late June recruitment had intensified to where Akoy wrote, "When you wake up from a very very long nap and you check your phone and have 10 missed calls from different college coaches!!!" His Twitter feed was filled with pleas from partisans to choose their dear beloved school and cover it in glory. The online high school/college "recruitment" media were equally persistent. The attention exhilarated and exhausted Akoy, though he clung to his sense of humor:

Waking up and finding (Lotte's) dads car keys in my pocket! SMDH!!! He just might need them to go to work. #keyless

He visited the campuses of Kansas and Missouri and then was home for the July Fourth holiday.
"My mom about to have me cooking outside in this hot weather!"
To which a friend asked, "I thought you liked the hot weather?"
Akoy responded, "I use to. I think I'm Americanise now."
Throughout July he attended a camp in Philadelphia, a tournament in Milwaukee, and a tournament in Kansas City.

By early August Akoy's short list included Louisville, Georgetown, Connecticut, West Virginia, and Southern California. His slightly longer list also included Marquette, Xavier, Clemson, Florida, Tennessee, and the two local schools, Nebraska and Creighton.

The choice weighed on Akoy; he knew how transformative it could be for himself and his family. Success in college could lead to the pot of gold otherwise known as the National Basketball Association. In the 2011–12 season ten NBA players had salaries above $18 million, with Kobe Bryant's $25.2 million at the top. Akoy's role model, LeBron James, made $16 million. Luol Deng, his fellow countryman, made $12.3 million. Within a year the average NBA salary would be $5.15 million. Within four years the league would have $24 billion in television contracts, while James's salary would be $23 million and his annual income with endorsements would be $71 million. The NBA's ten highest-paid players would bank $391 million from salaries and endorsements, with 46 percent of the total earned off the court. Much of the endorsement bonanza came from three shoe-and-apparel giants—Adidas, Nike, and Under Armour—whose combined sales were more than $25 billion by 2013.

NBA minimum salary for a rookie in 2012 was $490,180, or roughly what Akoy's father, Madut, could earn in fifteen years at the meat plant. After a year the minimum jumped to $788,872. The average ticket price for the Sacramento Kings, who in their distant past had played in Omaha, was $48. Add in parking, beer, and hot dogs, and the cost for two to attend a game equaled a day on the production line for Madut—which was a deal compared to the $99 average ticket price for the Los Angeles Lakers.

No mystery then why the NBA called to Akoy. Even one year at minimum salary would gain his family security. Pro leagues in Europe and Asia paid between $25,000 and $100,000. The proven route to all or any of it was through college. Akoy needed a program in which he could mature and develop and a coach he believed in and could trust.

That was the problem. More than a few college basketball coaches fell between "oily" and "slippery" on the trust scale. Some tripped on a dense thicket of NCAA regulations set up to preserve the "amateur" status of "student-athletes" and encourage competitive parity. Others knew exactly what they were doing when they skirted the rules. Bottom line: a lot of money was to be made by coaches who could win.

The NCAA business model of amateurism was a bonanza for coaches. Even as it imposed what amounted to a salary cap on "student-athletes"—a scholarship—coaches (and athletic directors) had no limitation on what they could earn. Flush with an $11 billion broadcast deal from CBS and Turner Sports, coaches cashed in.

In 2013 Louisville's Rick Pitino would make just shy of $5 million a year, a bit less than cross-state rival John Calipari's $5.4 million at Kentucky. The average pay for thirty-seven coaches in the 2012 March Madness was $1.57 million. Average pay a year later would be $1.75 million. Athletic directors shared in the largesse, with Tom Jurich's $1.4 million salary at Louisville atop the heap. The median pay of head football and basketball coaches rose about 100 percent between 2005–6 and 2011–12, compared with a 4 percent median rise for full professors at doctoral universities, according to the American Association of University Professors.

Amateurism was so lucrative it incentivized a culture of deception. Some of the coaches and colleges in pursuit of Akoy were part of it. Connecticut head coach Jim Calhoun, who was about to retire, was suspended for three games in 2011–12 for recruiting violations. West Virginia coach Bob Huggins, as head coach of Kansas State in 2007, was alleged in a lawsuit to have overseen illegal inducements in the recruitment of Michael Beasley. Southern California vacated all of its wins from 2007–8 after it was revealed that O. J. Mayo had received improper benefits. Tennessee was hit with a two-year probation in 2011 for numerous violations incurred by head coach Bruce Pearl. Marquette would suspend head coach Buzz Williams and fire one of his assistants before the 2012–13 season for recruiting violations.

Recruiting scandals had brought down Florida in the 1980s and Clemson in the 1990s. Memphis, with Calipari as head coach, vacated its 2007–8 season because Derrick Rose's entrance exam was fraudulent and the team had paid for Rose's brother to attend road games. Baylor plunged into scandal in 2003 after the murder of a player, Patrick Dennehy, by his teammate, Carlton Dotson, led to revelations of improper payments to players by head coach Dave Bliss. The NCAA put Baylor on probation from 2005 to 2010.

Louisville's program under Pitino, so far, was cleaner than his personal life. In 2010 a Kentucky woman was convicted of extortion in demanding millions of dollars from Pitino to keep secret their sexual encounter at a Louisville restaurant in 2003. Pitino, who was married, apologized publicly for his "poor judgment." Nothing equivalent yet had befallen Pitino's basketball program, which would go on to win the national championship in 2013. But that would change when allegations would surface in 2015 that between 2010 and 2014 Pitino's director of operations, Andre McGee, had paid for sex-and-stripper parties for recruits. In February 2018 the NCAA would vacate Louisville's 2013 championship because of the sex scandal. By that time Pitino had been fired for yet another scandal: a bribery-and-fraud scheme in which his program was alleged to have illegally funneled money to recruits through his shoe-and-apparel partner, Adidas.

As Akoy looked for a coach and program to trust, he might well have turned homeward, where the Nebraska and Creighton programs were clean, for the most part. Creighton was the choice of Akoy's mother because its campus was a five-minute walk. Many local fans urged Akoy to take his talent to Lincoln to help new coach Tim Miles. A follower had tweeted in July, "Come on @CoachMiles! Can't lose @ZerotheHeroAkoy to Gtown. Would be a tough blow to take." He had detractors too; a few claimed he was overrated and suggested that he had benefited from affirmative action, claims that got under his skin. "Haters Gonna Hate!" Akoy wrote. "Out to prove them wrong!!"

But neither Nebraska nor Creighton courted Akoy with the urgency he and Hammer considered his due. Miles squandered the capital his predecessor, Kenneth "Doc" Sadler, had built with Akoy. At the onset of the April recruiting period Miles had made his first visit to a prospect in New Zealand. Hammer thought Akoy should have been the priority. "I would have had the pep band in front of Akoy's house at midnight—whatever you can do to show interest," Hammer recalled. "He never even called to set up a home visit. I don't know if they didn't want him or if they thought they would get him like it was a no-brainer."

Akoy was cordial with the staff and players at Creighton because he had spent long hours at the Creighton gym. He had a cordial relationship with head coach Greg McDermott. That changed after an offhand comment Akoy made to media when asked about the hiring of Miles by Nebraska. "He told the reporter that Miles was a good hire for Nebraska," Hammer recalled. "Then he was asked about Creighton, and Akoy said, 'Well, there is another D-1 school in the state.' A few days later he was playing with Creighton's guys, and McDermott walked into the gym and just chewed his butt about the comment."

Even before the outburst Akoy had doubts about playing in McDermott's system, designed for his son Doug's considerable talent. McDermott's infrequent presence at Akoy's summer games sent a signal, and then too geography was an issue. Creighton was close to home—claustrophobia close. "It was better Akoy got away from home," Leisha Hammer said. "From his mom's cultural perspective Akoy was expected to have a greater role in the household. But from an American cultural perspective we wanted Akoy to get a great education. Being too close to home wouldn't have been fair to Akoy."

Creighton's fate may have been sealed one August dawn when Akoy was awakened by a tirade from his mother, who was on the phone with his father in Iowa. She hung up, stormed into his room, complained bitterly about her marriage, and warned Akoy not to turn out like his father.

At 6:05 a.m. Akoy wrote, "When your mom wake you up at 5 in the morning to give a speech!! #idiot thankful they won't be a part of making my college decision! #relief."

Temptation and Decision   **14**

What happened next was as old and new as creation: an apple disguised as a basketball tempted Akoy. It pitted him against just about everybody he loved and revered and tested his judgment and principles in a trial without a courtroom. "Akoy versus The People," he called it.

In the third week of August 2012 Akoy called Behrens with stunning news: he was about to transfer to a private prep school for his senior year. The school, Montrose Christian in Rockville, Maryland, had 370 students and an ambitious basketball program that had sent numerous players to colleges and a few to the NBA, most notably Kevin Durant. The small campus featured a dingy gym that seated fewer than six hundred, but its coach, Stu Vetter, attracted talent and thrived despite high roster turnover. Several Montrose Christian players had befriended Akoy on the summer grassroots circuit and urged him to transfer. The prep school cum basketball factory became the serpent in Akoy's garden.

The final decision would be made within a few days. Incredible as it seemed, Akoy was prepared to walk away from his prophecy of "Four" just one season short of fruition. Behrens did not doubt that Akoy might leave because he sensed what bubbled beneath the surface. "His mom and dad weren't getting along, and he and his mom butted heads a lot," Behrens recalled. "As kids get older, they want to get out and spread their wings. His mom had expectations for him to be there and provide. When his dad was gone, he had to be head of the household. He was tired of that and just wanted to be a high school kid. Maybe on the East Coast he could just be a kid. There was some escapism in this."

An escape to Maryland might also relieve Akoy's predicament with young women. There was Lotte, and then there was the pack of she-wolves in hot pursuit. Sometimes they misconstrued his affable manner as flirtation, which touched off speculation and rumor, which inevitably got back to Lotte. Early in August he wrote, "I hate girls sometimes. They can tell you one thing, but turn around and do something else!!" Akoy recalled, "I would meet a girl for the first time and be nice and smile, and she would go off and say, 'Akoy talked to me and winked at me' and add on all this extra fluff that didn't even happen. And then 'whoa, whoa, whoa,' something gets added along the way and it gets back to Lotte, and she says, 'I heard this and ten people said it. How can I believe you if ten people said it?' If ten people said something, it makes it more true, right? I promise you I met that person one time, and somehow this emerged. A lot of my time was trying to defend myself."

Other seductions called to Akoy. Montrose Christian claimed it would introduce him to a higher caliber of opponent, which would elevate his performance and marketability. Its media market, Washington-Baltimore, was ten times larger than Omaha. "He could improve his brand and label; I know that's what he was thinking," recalled teammate Tre'Shawn Thurman.

Then there was the "Christian" in Montrose Christian. Akoy was a pious Catholic and a regular at confession. Throughout his grassroots basketball travels he had sought out Sunday morning church services and had read a daily verse from the Bible. "Basketball takes me away from the church," he once wrote. "Without the Lord I wouldn't be who I am today." The stated mission of Montrose Christian was to provide "Christ-Centered education for the Glory of the Savior and the Good of Society." The tandem of religion and basketball was hard for Akoy to resist. "Why not go to a school where you get challenged every day, and all you do is school, basketball, school, basketball?" Akoy said. "No other, I don't want to say distractions, but [no] other things going on."

Behrens understood the forces at play and knew well the stress of marriage, but he wasn't about to hold the door open and wave good-bye. He asked Akoy to put off his decision until they could talk again. Then he huddled with Bigsby, the principal, and the two hatched a plan to talk Akoy off the ledge, so to speak, to keep him at Central. Behrens would handle the basketball side of the effort and Bigsby the academic.

Soon enough Akoy came to Bigsby's office with a document to formalize the transfer. He told Bigsby he planned to visit Montrose Christian, with Dave Sjulin, the next week. He planned to stay if he liked it, and if he stayed, he would need a transfer form signed by Bigsby. But his hope of mute compliance was quickly dashed. Bigsby did not do mute.

"What do you know about Montrose?"

"It's got a good basketball program."

"I don't care about that. What about academics?"

For the first time, but not the last, Akoy felt like he was on trial. He had no answer for Bigsby. "I'm not signing anything," Bigsby said. "Why would I let you go to an inferior institution and jeopardize your academic future for what—basketball?"

Akoy's bile rose as Bigsby picked up his phone, called Montrose Christian, and asked for the assistant basketball coach who had recruited Akoy. When the man was on the line, Bigsby peppered him with questions.

"I asked about the AP classes they offered," Bigsby recalled. "They offered one, AP Spanish. Akoy was enrolled in three and we offered several more.

"I went down the list of what we offered: our broad range of courses, teachers' tenure, after-school clubs, IB program. They had none of it. I asked how many National Merit scholars they had. None. I was killing him. He said I was being judgmental. I told him he had no business recruiting my student. He said he would find another way around me. Finally I told him, 'Don't you come anywhere near this school.'"

Bigsby hung up and turned to Akoy, who was livid.

"This place has a website; that's what it boils down to," Bigsby said. "Why would you go there?"

"Kevin Durant went there. He's got a million dollars in the bank."

"If you want to measure a school by successful alumni, I'd put our Alumni Wall against theirs any day of the week."

Within a day or two the news reached Akoy's teammates. "My first thought was, 'Forget him; we're gonna win the state championship with or without him," Tra-Deon Hollins recalled. "But then reality set in, and I thought, 'He can't leave. We can't do it ourselves. We need him.'"

Tre'Shawn Thurman recalled, "I was disappointed first that I didn't hear it from him, and I was disappointed that he was even thinking about it. We had been through so much; we had built a relationship. A bunch of us began to talk because if it was a reality, we had to change roles." Thurman texted an urgent plea: "Hey man we need you. We play some great teams this year and go to some great places too. You didn't win three in a row for nothing. You got to finish it." Akoy texted back: "I'm thinking." Thurman backed off. "I let him be in his own little world," he recalled. "I didn't want to push him away."

By Saturday, August 18, when local media ran with the story, Behrens had arranged to meet with Akoy, the Sjulins, and Scott Hammer. He showed up at the Sjulins' home with a thick folder on Montrose Christian. His research attacked a couple of misconceptions. "Montrose touted that their players went to high D-1 programs," recalled Dave Sjulin. "Eric had stats that showed where they really went and that it was comparable to where Eric's players went."

Behrens was most persuasive when it came to schedules and caliber of opponent. "Akoy thought they played a national schedule," Behrens recalled. "I pulled up the schedule. They had one decent trip. Basically they played a bunch of overmatched private schools and a DC schedule no stronger than the best teams in Omaha. There was no Oak Hill, St. Anthony's, or Montverde Academy. He was a little surprised. He thought it would be travel and games around the country."

Meanwhile, Central was scheduled for the City of Palms tournament in Fort Myers, Florida, in December, against some of the best teams in the country. In February it was matched against vaunted Oak Hill Academy in a showdown at Grand Island, Nebraska. "He [Behrens] showed us that Montrose Christian's level of opposition wasn't appreciably different than what Akoy would experience at Central," Dave Sjulin recalled.

Behrens urged Akoy, the Sjulins, and Hammer to consider what Akoy would leave behind. "I told them that kids who leave for prep schools usually are struggling," Behrens recalled. "Akoy was thriving. It was strange for a kid in a good environment with a strong support system and teachers who had his back to think about leaving. Basketball aside, Akoy was in a good place from eight to three. He couldn't have gone to a better high school to prepare for college." Behrens finished with a plea to Akoy's self-narrative: "One more title and your legacy will be cemented," he said. "Don't you want to finish up what you started?"

At the start of the meeting Akoy thought Montrose Christian had the support of at least one adult, Dave Sjulin, whose faith inclined him toward private religious schools. Sjulin had bought two airplane tickets to take Akoy to Maryland. Behrens had Sjulin in mind when he said, "Not every school with 'Christian' in its title has a religious curriculum. . . . That's not the right reason to be making a change." Sjulin flipped, and Akoy realized he was on his own. Now truly it was "Akoy versus The People."

Akoy went home with a lot to think about. What did he owe his mother and siblings with his father absent much of the time? He shuddered to imagine the household without his steady hand. What did he owe his coaches and teammates? They were family too, and their hoop dreams were hitched to him. What did he owe his high school, which had secured its stature with his help? If he left, even Bigsby would be hard-pressed to put a positive spin on his departure. How much would he miss his extended family of Lotte, the Sjulins, and the Hammers? From a business perspective what if Behrens was right? What if another season with Central, and a potential fourth title, could do more for his brand than Montrose Christian? At bottom was the question of identity. What part of him was still a nomadic refugee? What part a rooted Nebraskan? What part teen drama king? Was he someone who ran from his problems, or confronted them?

Thoughts churned and sleep was elusive. At 2:33 a.m. on Sunday, August 19, Akoy tweeted:

Got to go to #Church in the morning!!
Hopefully #God can help me with this decision!!!

True to his tweet and habit, Akoy went to church and prayed for guidance. Sunday afternoon at a Team Nebraska Express picnic he told Hammer of his decision. Then he called Behrens. "I'm staying," he said. "It's not what I thought it was." A day later local and basketball media reported he would stay, and just like that, the serpent was vanquished and Montrose Christian slithered into the murk. Omaha had Akoy back, and those close to him exhaled. "That four in a row meant a lot to him; it might have been the decider," said Thurman, his teammate. "He didn't win three in a row for nothing. He started it, and he wanted to finish it."

Still the college decision hung over Akoy's head. Dave Sjulin had two tickets from the canceled trip to Maryland that he now used to take Akoy to Georgetown. Akoy met with head coach John Thompson III and toured the facilities, which included a modest weight room. Akoy recalled Thompson's words: "This was good enough for Patrick Ewing; you don't need all that fancy stuff. We can make you an NBA big man, but you've got to do the work." Thompson told Akoy he had seen him play at an AAU tournament in Arkansas. "A lot of times it's my assistants who pick who we go after," Thompson said. "But I found you."

Thompson had little of the scowling righteousness that defined his father and namesake, John Thompson Jr., who had coached Georgetown from 1972 to 1999 and won the national title in 1984. Akoy liked Thompson and that Georgetown had developed big men for the NBA—Ewing, Dikembe Mutombo, Alonzo Mourning, Roy Hibbert, and Greg Monroe, to name a few. Thompson seemed to like Akoy—just not enough to visit him in Omaha a few days later. Instead he sent an assistant coach to meet with Akoy, Adaw, Hammer, and the Sjulins. Akoy had expected to welcome Thompson and to commit to Georgetown, but now he held off. Louisville was worth a look, particularly because its up-tempo high-pressure style, as coached by Rick Pitino, mirrored Behrens's system at Central.

In mid-September Akoy and Hammer visited Louisville. Akoy was squired on campus by Louisville's 6-foot-11 center, Gorgui Dieng, a native of Senegal. He went to a football practice and game, attended a volleyball game, and dined with Pitino's assistants. One of Pitino's assistants, Kareem

Richardson, had spotted Akoy as a ninth-grader at a camp in Iowa and had put him on Louisville's radar.

After dinner Saturday Hammer turned in, and Akoy went out with his hosts. This was the period when recruits allegedly had sex with escorts hired and paid by Louisville director of operations Andre McGee. The allegations surfaced in a 2015 book, *Breaking Cardinal Rules: Basketball and the Escort Queen*, by Katina Powell, a prostitute by trade. The book opened with Powell's statement, "I felt like I was part of the recruitment team. A lot of them players went to Louisville because of me." She claimed to have arranged for escorts to have sex with recruits and players on a couple of dozen occasions, at the players' dorm, and that McGee had paid her more than $10,000 in total.

Akoy was not among the several recruits and players Powell named. When the scandal broke in late 2015, he made no statement to local or basketball media or on his social media, even though speculation was rife. Kareem Richardson, who recruited Akoy, left Louisville in 2013 to become head coach at the University of Missouri–Kansas City (UMKC). After the scandal broke, Andre McGee was fired by Pitino and hired by Richardson at UMKC. Whatever happened in Louisville, if anything, stayed in Louisville. (My question to Akoy received a "no comment.") Akoy and Hammer returned to Omaha, and Akoy went back to Central. Three days later Pitino and Richardson came to the Sjulins' home to close the deal. They dined on lasagna with Akoy, Adaw, Behrens, the Hammers, and the Sjulins, including Lotte. "It's pretty powerful when Rick Pitino shows up at your house," Leisha Hammer recalled.

Akoy managed to push away his favorite dish to listen to Pitino, who carried most of the conversation, about his program and himself, minus the salacious parts. He was married with five children, and a sixth had died in infancy. He had grown up on Long Island and played basketball at the University of Massachusetts–Amherst. He had coached at Boston University and Providence, where he lost in the Final Four in 1987, and Kentucky, where he won the 1996 national title and lost in the 1997 final. He had had mixed success as coach of the New York Knicks (1987–89) and notable failure as coach of the Boston Celtics (1997–2001), which he skirted without mention of his infamous rant about Boston: "All the negativity that's in this town sucks. I've been around when Jim Rice was booed. I've been around when [Carl] Yastrzemski was booed. And it stinks. It makes the greatest town, greatest city in the world, lousy."

Hired by Louisville in 2001, Pitino lost his brother-in-law and close friend, Billy Minardi, a bond trader, in the 9/11 attacks on the World Trade Center. He took the Cardinals to the Final Four in 2005 and again in the spring of 2012. He spoke of Louisville's proud tradition and his optimism for the coming season. He hoped Akoy would choose Louisville and add to the tradition.

That was it. Pitino and Richardson rose, thanked their hosts, and headed for the door. It was then that Akoy rose and followed Pitino to the door, with Leisha Hammer a step behind.

"Coach, I know it was your birthday yesterday, and I have a late present for you," Akoy said. Pitino stopped in his tracks.

Leisha hissed, "Do not commit. You don't have to make a decision tonight." Akoy could not resist. He had seen too many films. This was his Gipper moment: "Next year I'll be attending University of Louisville."

Pitino beamed and wrapped Akoy in a hug as the room lost its collective breath. As several who were there remembered it, Pitino said, "Wow, it's a great year to be sixty."

A loud keening wail broke the silence. "All you could hear was this high-pitched 'wooooo,'" Scott Hammer recalled.

Lotte unleashed, as Akoy put it, "a flood of tears." She had wanted Akoy to go to Nebraska, where she was headed to play softball. Pitino recognized the anguish of a broken heart and said to her, "You can come to Louisville, too. It's a public school."

In fading September light Akoy had picked a college after he had served guests lasagna. Now he made one more decision: to put his arm around Lotte and comfort her.

Standing Bear and Brando   **15**

Akoy was an insider now, with perks and benefits. As a senior the Central High Foundation (CHSF) hired him at ten dollars an hour to stuff envelopes and chat up alumni at the downtown office and at fundraisers. Executive director Michele Roberts recalled, "I got a call from Keith Bigsby and Eric Behrens asking me to find him work at our office. It was when he was looking at that [prep] school out east. They had promised him money to financially take care of his family. Obviously CHSF couldn't do that, but we offered him a job so he could earn a paycheck to help with his family's finances."

Adaw's washing machine broke, Roberts recalled, and Akoy was set to replace it with his first paycheck when alum retail magnates Nelson and Linda Gordman gifted her one. "That way Akoy could use his money for other family necessities," Roberts said. "It was a culture thing. His mom felt he should be helping to contribute to his family's financial situation. . . . In the end he was a hard worker and worked well with our other student workers. There was more than one occasion when Eric kicked him out of practice and Akoy would show up at our office saying he was going to work." He got himself kicked out, she recalled, "because he always wanted the last word or he went through the motions half-assed." Roberts would drag him back to the gym and have him apologize to Behrens.

The Jewish Community Center gave Akoy part-time work in its youth basketball program. He became co-president of his favorite club, FBLA. The Sjulins gave him the use of their eldest daughter's Hyundai after she went abroad to study. The car enabled him to work late at CHSF (where he had his own key), help his mother transport his younger siblings, and navigate the city at his convenience, all with the assurance that a full scholarship awaited him upon graduation.

STANDING BEAR AND BRANDO

Yet even as the system nurtured him, Akoy had doubts. America held out a hand to refugees, sure, but it was slippery, and the ground below was hard. On the day of the presidential election in November 2012, which would give Barack Obama a second term, he wrote, "Truthfully I'm just mad I can't run for president cause I was born in Africa! #ConstitutionChange US ran by Akoy sounds pretty good! #real."

A year before Akoy had unleashed a sarcastic tweet at the Department of Motor Vehicles because its database did not list him as a citizen. The digital error was offensive, Akoy recalled, because "I felt like that just put me in a box: 'Oh well, he's not a citizen; he's in this other category.' I didn't like being othered."

No surprise then that Akoy took special interest in two senior courses that spoke to his refugee experience. One was Holocaust Literature, taught by Jen Stastny, who had met Akoy as a freshman and knew him as well as any teacher. "I'm sure he pulled strings to get in my class," Stastny recalled. "He could do that. He was charming, bright, a star. He could get people to do what he wanted."

Holocaust Literature examined primary source documents as well as memoirs, such as *All but My Life*, by Gerda Weissmann Klein, a Polish Jew who had survived six years in Nazi concentration and work camps with "positivity and imagination to keep hope alive." Students were assigned to write about Holocaust rescuers or about rescuers in other historical events who showed moral courage.

"Akoy loved that book—he related it to his time in Egypt; that's what he remembered most," Stastny recalled. "He talked about being treated badly there for being black. His immigrant experience of moving from place to place seemed to inform him of people who didn't belong in their own place. That and also his religion made him think about how to live a good life and be an ethical person. His Catholicism was very conservative, very much the words of Jesus: Love thy neighbor."

Akoy's cultural and religious backgrounds were evident in his classroom demeanor, Stastny recalled. "He was disgusted with kids who didn't respect themselves or their elders and also [didn't] respect the people in the stories we read," Stastny said. "One boy was really negative and tried to show off, and Akoy didn't put up with that kid being disrespectful to me. I had to tell Akoy I could fight my own fights, that I'd been around for a long time. He would treat me like a mom or sister, listen to me and respect me, but also want to take care of me. Part of it was culture—he definitely had to take care of his mom, and he was responsible for his siblings because his dad was away. Also his religion was key to how he believed he should treat women. He struggled with me because I'm not religious, and I'm super-independent and pretty defiant. He would say, 'Miss Stastny you have to stop.' I would say, 'I don't have to do anything. I can do what I want. I'm the teacher.'

"As a senior Akoy was more mature than the other kids around him. Maybe that was a function of the roles he had at home and also of Lotte. When he started dating her, he really aspired to be stable and respectable and dignified. And yet he was still kind of a baby in many ways. He would stay after school and try to convince me to do his work for him. I would tell him, 'Shut up and leave. You can have my time, but I won't do your work for you.'"

The other senior course Akoy favored was Omaha History, which introduced him to a nineteenth-century refugee whose quest for justice climaxed down the street from Central. Standing Bear was a Native American Ponca chief whose life, Akoy had to concede, was even more dramatic than his own. His story held up a distant mirror to Akoy's people in South Sudan and to Akoy. Jay Ball, who taught Omaha History, said Standing Bear "resonates with many of my students on a personal level."

The Ponca were a peaceful tribe of about eight hundred who hunted and farmed in northeastern Nebraska. Standing Bear, known to the Ponca as Ma-chu-nah-zah, was born in 1829 and became a chief at an early age because of his leadership abilities. Legend held that his prayers once diverted a powerful storm that threatened to disrupt a sacred dance. In the 1850s the U.S. government began to pressure the Ponca to cede their land along the Niobrara River to accommodate white settlers. In 1875 the government manufactured an agreement to move the Ponca to Indian Territory in Oklahoma, though the Ponca had not agreed.

In May 1877 the Ponca, then essentially refugees, were sent to Indian Territory, where harsh conditions and lack of basic supplies resulted in 158 deaths, or about one-fourth the tribe, within a year and a half. Early in 1879 Standing Bear resolved to return to the Niobrara to bury his teenage son's remains. On their journey home, in the depth of winter, he and twenty-seven other Ponca were arrested at the Omaha Reservation and jailed at Fort Omaha. Standing Bear's plight aroused the sympathy of the commander of Fort Omaha, Gen. George Crook, and an Omaha newspaperman, Thomas Tibbles. They believed Standing Bear's rights had been abridged under the Fourteenth Amendment, passed in 1868 to prohibit slavery, and determined that Standing Bear should sue the federal government. They got a federal judge in Omaha, Elmer Dundy, to allow a lawsuit to proceed, which in itself set a precedent.

Two prominent Omaha attorneys, John Lee Webster and Andrew Jackson Poppleton, agreed to represent Standing Bear pro bono. The two-day trial began on May 1, 1879, at the courthouse at Fifteenth and Dodge, five blocks from Central High, then known as Omaha High. On the first day Standing Bear testified, through a translator, and contrasted the plentiful life of the Ponca in Nebraska with their suffering in Indian Territory. On the second day plaintiff attorney Webster focused on the intent of the Fourteenth Amendment—to promote and protect individual liberties. The amendment, Webster argued, applied to Standing Bear and the Ponca, and it made "an Indian who was born in this country and who did not owe allegiance to any other form of government a citizen beyond all dispute." In response the government attorney argued that "the Indian—as far as the law was concerned—was neither a citizen nor a person, and so he couldn't bring a suit of any kind against the government of the United States." The government argued that Judge Dundy had erred in permitting Standing Bear's lawsuit.

Rebuttal came from Standing Bear's other attorney, Poppleton, who argued that U.S. laws must extend to Native American tribes, that they were not wards of the government, and that they most certainly had rights. To deny Standing Bear the right to sue, he argued, was to deny he was a human. Poppleton recounted Standing Bear's vow to bury his son in his old home.

"That man not a human being?" said Poppleton. "Who of all [of] us would have done it? Look around this city and State and find, if you can, the man who has gathered up the ashes of his dead, wandered for sixty days through a strange country without guide or compass, aided by the sun and stars only, that the bones of that kindred may be buried in the land of their birth. No! It is a libel upon religion; it is a libel upon missionaries who sacrifice so much and risk their lives in order to take to these Indians that gospel which Christ proclaimed to all the wide earth, to say that these are not human beings."

By the time Poppleton finished, court had been in session for twelve hours. Before adjournment Judge Dundy announced that Standing Bear wished to address the court. In a climactic moment, Standing Bear went to the front of the courtroom and faced the audience. He extended his right hand and held it for all to see and then turned to the judge and spoke, his words conveyed by a translator. "That hand is not the color of yours, but if I pierce it, I shall feel pain," Standing Bear said. "If you pierce your hand, you also feel pain. The blood that will flow from mine will be of the same color as yours. I am a man. The same God made us both."

History does not say if Standing Bear knew of Shylock's soliloquy in Shakespeare's *Merchant of Venice*—"Hath not a Jew eyes? Hath not a Jew hands, organs, dimensions, senses, affections, passions? . . . If you prick us do we not bleed?"—but he had delivered a Native American version. Many in the courtroom were brought to tears, and even the judge and General Crook were visibly moved.

Judge Dundy gave his verdict ten days later. The Fourteenth Amendment, indeed, gave Standing Bear the right to expatriate himself from his tribe and from Indian Territory. The government had no legal right to send him back to Indian Territory. He concluded: "An Indian is a PERSON within the meaning of the laws of the United States, and has therefore the right to sue out a writ of habeas corpus in a federal court." The Ponca had been illegally detained in violation of their constitutional rights and "must be discharged from custody, and it is so ordered."

Thus with a stroke of the judge's pen, the Ponca were transformed from refugees into citizens. Standing Bear buried his son near his home on the Niobrara. He toured the East Coast as a lecturer on Native American rights, and after prolonged legalities over who owned what and how much, he lived next to the Niobrara until his death in 1908.

More than 130 years later Standing Bear's landmark case inspired Akoy in Central's Omaha History class. "It's a story of injustice, resolve, perseverance, love for family, and ultimately the recognition that we are all humans, and despite some external differences, we are similar in our pursuits," Ball said. "I am sure Akoy was able to relate many of his own life experiences to the plight of the Ponca."

Standing Bear's legacy had a special connection to Central, and oddly enough, to Hollywood. In the late 1890s Standing Bear's attorney John Lee Webster hired as a secretary Bess Pennebaker, a young widow and mother. Webster's progressive causes—civil rights for immigrants and blacks and voting rights for women—became Bess Pennebaker's as well. She married an Omaha businessman, Frank Myers, and in 1912 enrolled her daughter, Dorothy "Dodie" Pennebaker Myers, at Central. As a fifteen-year-old Dodie Myers fell in love with seventeen-year-old Marlon Brando, who also may have attended Central, though he was not a graduate.

Dodie graduated from Central in 1916, married Marlon in 1918, lived on the West Coast for a time, and returned to Omaha in 1922. Their third child, Marlon Brando Jr., was born in 1924. Dodie shared her mother's passion for reform—of child labor laws, education of unwed mothers, health and safety standards, and working conditions for migrants—and when her pet issues were on the ballot, she handed out pamphlets and gave speeches.

Dodie struggled with alcoholism, which stained Marlon Jr.'s childhood. But she handed down to him the social conscience of her mother, as well as the acting bug. Dodie Brando was a mainstay at the Omaha Community Playhouse, founded in 1924, where she starred in its first play, *The*

Enchanted Cottage, in 1925. The cast included Jayne Fonda, whose brother Henry Fonda was a 1923 graduate of Central. Dodie recruited Henry to play the juvenile lead for *You and I*, to open the 1925–26 season; it helped launch him as one of the most iconic actors of the twentieth century. Fonda played opposite Dodie in *Beyond the Horizon*, for which she won rave reviews. When Dodie Brando and her family moved to Illinois in 1930, she left an indelible imprint on the playhouse. In 1930 Henry Fonda returned to guest star in *A Kiss for Cinderella* alongside thirteen-year-old Dorothy McGuire, who was a freshman at Central and who went on to a distinguished career on Broadway and in Hollywood.

For his part, Marlon Brando Jr. went on to become one of the most influential and eccentric actors of the twentieth century. He won his first Academy Award for Best Actor for his role as dockworker Terry Malloy in the 1954 film *On the Waterfront*. In the drama about corruption in New York's longshoremen's union, Malloy is called upon to testify against the mob-connected union boss and wrestles with the decision to be a "rat." Director Elia Kazan wrote the film as an allegory and critique of the "blacklist" that sought to root out alleged Communists from Hollywood in the postwar years and to expel writers, directors, and actors as refugees of a sort. The progenitor of the "blacklist," the House Un-American Activities Committee (HUAC), would come to be seen as an assault on the democratic values it claimed to represent.

The role of Malloy was in Brando's political wheelhouse, as he embraced the politics of tolerance and inclusion taught him by his mother and grandmother, and he was public about it. In 1963 he participated in a Freedom Ride in the Deep South and in the March on Washington, where he stood on the dais with Martin Luther King. In the late 1960s he gave money to the Black Panther Party.

In the early 1970s Brando took up the cause of the American Indian Movement (AIM) in a karmic link to Standing Bear. When Brando won his second Academy Award for Best Actor in 1973 for his role as Vito Corleone in *The Godfather*, he famously used the Academy Awards ceremony to protest the ongoing siege at Wounded Knee, South Dakota, and Hollywood's historical "defamation" of Native Americans. He sent as his proxy Sacheen Little Feather, an actress with Native American lineage, to deliver a statement he wrote. The show's producer prevented Little Feather, who appeared in traditional Apache attire, from reading the full four-page statement on camera. Instead, as Brando wrote in his autobiography, "Under great pressure she had to ad-lib a few words on behalf of the American Indian, and it made me proud of her. I don't know what happened to that Oscar. The Motion Picture Academy may have sent it to me, but if it did I don't know where it is now." Brando's autobiography, published in 1994, was titled *Brando: Songs My Mother Taught Me*.

Standing Bear's and Brando's legacy rolled forward. John Trudell, a Santee Sioux born in Omaha and raised near the Ponca ancestral lands, was an activist and national chairman of the AIM from 1973 to 1979. In the 1980s and 1990s Trudell was a poet, musician, actor, and eloquent voice for Native American identity and pride. Along the way he met actress Marcheline Bertrand, with whom he shared a relationship.

In the late 1990s Bertrand's daughter, Angelina Jolie, rose to stardom as an actress. Her career took off in 1999, when she won the Best Supporting Actress award for her role as a mental patient in *Girl, Interrupted*. In 2000, while filming *Lara Croft: Tomb Raider* in Cambodia, she learned of the Khmer Rouge genocide of the late 1970s, and it sparked her concern for refugees. Early in 2001 Jolie approached UNHCR and expressed her desire to help. She paid for field trips to refugee camps in Chad, Sierra Leone, Tanzania, Cambodia, and Pakistan, and in August 2001 UNHCR gave her the honorary title of Goodwill Ambassador.

Trudell and Bertrand pulled Jolie toward the Native American movement as her activism expanded. At one point Jolie enlisted Trudell's help to adopt a Native American child but dropped the effort due to lineage rules. In 2002 she financed the start-up of a philanthropic nonprofit, All Tribes Foundation, which her mother ran and for which Trudell served as a "creative adviser." Jolie also financed Trudell's 2002 album, *Bone Days*, and was an executive producer of the 2005 film documentary *Trudell*.

Throughout the 2000s Jolie used her box office fame to draw attention to the plight of refugees in her field missions to more than thirty countries, including Sudan. She adopted children from Cambodia, Ethiopia, and Vietnam and gave birth to three. UNHCR promoted Jolie to the rank of Special Envoy in April 2012 and authorized her to meet with diplomats and global leaders.

In her 2003 book, *Notes from My Travels*, Jolie wrote, "I honestly believe that if we were all aware, we would be compelled to act. So the question is not how or why I would do this with my life. The question is, how could I not?"

Dynasty Blues

16

Hoosiers is a 1986 film about a fictional town in Hickory, Indiana, whose basketball team is led by a new coach with a checkered past, a role played by Gene Hackman. Against all odds, Hickory upsets the defending champions from South Bend to win the 1954 state title.

The film is based on an actual small town in southeast Indiana, Milan, whose team upset the perennial champion, Muncie Central, in the 1954 state final. In those days all Indiana high schools, large and small, competed in one tournament, and South Bend and Muncie were large. Milan High had an enrollment of 162; Muncie Central, 1,662.

Hoosiers is David versus Goliath in high-tops. In the end almost everybody roots for Hickory (or Milan) as David. Almost nobody roots for South Bend (or Muncie Central) as Goliath. That's how it was for Omaha Central in the latter years of the Behrens dynasty. "A lot of times we felt like Muncie Central," Behrens recalled. "We were the bad guys in the movie, and most people rooted against us. That's natural; it's sports. Our job was to block that stuff out."

Behrens had a distant link to *Hoosiers* through Herb Welling, his volunteer assistant until 2009. Welling attended Mitchell High in Colorado Springs in the early 1980s, where his basketball coach, Bill Wright, mentored him. Wright had grown up in Indiana and had played on the 1953 Richmond Red Devils team that upset none other than defending champion Muncie Central in a regional final. Wright had a basement library of basketball books and films that Welling, who lived across the street, studied as a teenager. When Welling joined Behrens's staff in 2001, he brought along Wright's knowledge and Hoosier karma.

By the spring of 2012 Behrens had been in the Muncie/Goliath role long enough to feel trapped by it. Winning is supposed to be fun, but for Behrens and Central it had become obligatory. "When you're supposed to win, you breathe a sigh of relief and move on," Behrens recalled. "What you miss is the exhilaration."

While Central was respected within Nebraska basketball, it also was quietly resented. Metropolitan rivals believed its dynasty was built unfairly on the talent supplied by Scott Hammer and Welling and only grudgingly acknowledged Behrens as a team builder, strategist, conditioning guru, psychologist, and social worker. Online rumor mills targeted Central. "Those silly basketball websites wrote horrible things," recalled Rod Mullen. "Central gives players free cell phone minutes or Central allows players to not go to class and to commit crimes—outright lies or exaggerations. Posts would be anonymous, so we couldn't trace them. That's the kind of nonsense we had to deal with."

Behrens had coached Central to the state title in six of the last seven years. Most of his horses would be back from the 30–0 season, and he was about to get a blue-chip transfer, 6-foot-4 guard Nick Billingsley, from North High. Billingsley was a Hammer protégé, and his transfer would arouse the usual cynicism from rivals, even as he made Central a prohibitive favorite. His toughest opponents, Behrens foresaw, would be complacency and overconfidence.

Behrens's solution was to look for opponents outside of Nebraska, to whom Central's dynasty meant nothing and to whom Nebraska basketball meant even less. Nationally Nebraska was perceived as a football state. Evidence came from the basketball recruiting websites, which ranked the best players in each senior class. One established site, Rivals.com, named eight Nebraska prospects for 2013, with Akoy the highest-rated at four stars out of a possible five. None of the other prospects got a single star.

By comparison, among bordering states, Kansas had 47, Iowa 33, and Missouri 26 prospects. Indiana had 55 prospects, with 5 at four stars or five, and North Carolina had 60. Maryland had 63, two of which played for Montrose Christian, the prep school that had recruited Akoy. Virginia had 63, of which 5 played for Oak Hill Academy, a private prep school soon to become familiar to Nebraskans. Georgia had 85 prospects. Florida had 111, with 11 at four stars or five. California had 166, with 11 at four stars or five.

Population worked against Nebraska, its 1.82 million residents making it thirty-seventh among the fifty states (2010 census), while California had 37.2 million, or about twenty times more. Logically fewer residents would mean fewer prospects, except that Nebraska had fewer prospects per capita than a lot of states. Nebraska had nearly one-third the residents of Maryland and only one-eighth as many prospects. It had a bit more than one-fifth the population of Virginia and just one-eighth as many prospects. It had a bit less than 20 percent of Georgia's population and less than 10 percent as many prospects.

New Hampshire, with less than three-fourths the population of Nebraska, had twelve prospects, with two at four stars and two at five stars. New Hampshire's numbers were bolstered by private prep schools, such as Brewster Academy and New Hampton School, which had high-powered programs with a national reach. West Virginia, with roughly the same population as Nebraska, had eight prospects, seven of which came from the same private school, Huntington Prep, founded in 2009 as a "basketball-focused college preparatory school" in which "all students are considered D-1 prospects." Huntington Prep featured the No. 1–ranked prospect in the country, Andrew Wiggin, at five stars, and three players at four stars. Nebraska had nothing comparable.

The shoe-and-apparel companies Nike, Adidas, and Under Armour, ignored Nebraska's grassroots programs, as they lavished teams in Iowa, Missouri, and Kansas with sponsorship and merchandise. The lack of shoe sponsorship added to the perception of Nebraska as a football state.

Historically the contributions of Nebraska high schools to the NBA and defunct ABA were few and far between and from bygone eras: Bob Boozer (1950s), Ron Boone (1960s), Mike McGee (1970s), and Erick Strickland (1990s). Others peaked as NBA journeymen—Wally Anderzunas, Tom Kropp, Lee Johnson, Alex Stivrins, Bart Kofoed, Dave Hoppen, Rich King. A couple made brief cameos: Dwaine Dillard and Cedric Hunter. Strickland, a Bellevue West grad, was in the NBA from 1997 to 2005. No

Nebraska high school product had gone to the top after Strickland through the time of Akoy.

Akoy had won three straight championships in the large-school division and had been recruited by some of the top D-1 colleges in the country. He was Nebraska's first four-star player since Rivals.com started its rankings in 2002. Yet Rivals.com put him at No. 87 among its top 150 prospects, while ESPN had him at No. 75. His modest ranking reflected doubts about his offensive game, as well as about Nebraska. Central had finished a perfect 30–0 and won its third straight championship in 2011–12, yet MaxPreps.com had ranked it twentieth in the country, behind several teams with three or four losses and DeSoto, Texas, with six.

It was no small irony, Behrens realized, that while Central was Muncie in Nebraska, it was Milan on a national stage. He figured a few games against national powers could untangle this paradox. Was Central only good enough to win in Nebraska, or could it win anywhere? Was Nebraska basketball as irrelevant as the rest of the country seemed to think, or could it go against the best? Back in February 2006 Behrens had scheduled a private school from Louisiana, Reserve Christian, for a game in Omaha. That had gone badly, an 81–70 loss, though it catalyzed the team, which went on to win Behrens's first state title. Welling had urged Behrens to build a national schedule, but after he left, the idea lay fallow.

Now Behrens added two national components. The first was the City of Palms tournament in Fort Myers, Florida, in the week before Christmas. City of Palms, in its fortieth year, was a premier high school tournament, with a sixteen-team field of elite private schools and big-city powerhouses. The previous year eleven of the sixteen teams had gone on to win state championships. Its top seed, private Montverde Academy, was building a $6.5 million athletic complex at its campus near Orlando. "We knew it would be a great test to see how we stacked up," Behrens recalled. "I didn't know if we had the depth, if Akoy got in foul trouble, to match up. I knew we had six really good players, but our rotation stopped with six, in close games. That concerned me because we might have had to play four games in five days."

Akoy cut the ribbon at an October ceremony that made Central the first public school in Omaha to go completely wireless, the culmination of a million-dollar campaign by CHSF. That same month the *Register* profiled him with a spread that covered nearly two pages. He was a star who not only valued media, he cultivated it. "I can't count on one hand how many times Akoy was down in 029 (the *Register* office)," recalled editor-in-chief Jen Rooney. Yet Akoy set limits with the media. He agreed to a *Register* photo shoot in the gym with executive editor-in-chief Emily Beck, but when she asked him to recreate the signature "roar" that accompanied his dunks, he demurred. "He said it only happened in the moment," recalled Beck.

Signing day, when seniors committed with a letter, was in mid-November. The letter had seemed like a formality after Rick Pitino's visit in September, and it would have been had not Nebraska coach Tim Miles put on a late rush. Akoy was conflicted by Lotte's decision to attend Nebraska and Adaw's pleas to stay close, and he listened to Miles. Then Pitino jumped back in and persuaded Akoy to stick with Louisville, to the bitter disappointment of Husker fans on social media. "Sorry everyone that is mad that I made a decision that was going to benefit my life," Akoy wrote. "Didn't know that was a crime! Get on with your life!!!" He added: "People are so crazy!! . . People can say all they want but the people I love are happy for me. And that's all that matters."

Early in December Central opened its season. Several players—though not Akoy—colored their hair yellow to complement their neon socks and shoes and added theatrical dance moves to their introductions. Central won its first four games locally, as expected, and basketball seemed an afterthought to performance art. On December 18, as a blizzard bore down on Omaha, Akoy was in balmy Fort Myers. He posted a photo of a sumptuous breakfast spread and wrote, "Down in Florida just ate at the Waffle House! #livinggood." Lasagna was not in the photo, presumably because it wasn't on the breakfast menu.

When Central took the floor against a suburban Atlanta team, Eagle's Landing, it became the first basketball team from Nebraska to play in a boys' national high school invitational. Eagle's Landing was not the opponent Behrens had in mind. It too was making its first appearance in a national invitational tournament, and it was unranked in the national polls, while ESPN and MaxPreps had Central ranked at 22 and 13, respectively. Central found itself in the too familiar role as favorite and won easily, 62–37, behind Akoy's game-high 16 points. "We had to prove to ourselves that we belong here, so we came here with a mindset and a chip on our shoulder," Akoy told a reporter. The next day the *Naples Daily News* featured Akoy on the front of its sports section under the headline, "Sudanese Sensation." Central's victory was its forty-first straight, dating back to the 2010–11 season, tying it with Grand Island (1947–1949) for the longest win streak in Nebraska Class A history.

Next up was Long Beach Polytechnic, ranked No. 2 by MaxPreps and No. 8 by ESPN and *USA Today*. Long Beach Poly had five thousand students and a storied athletic tradition such that *Sports Illustrated* recognized it in 2005 as "Sports School of the Century." The California team featured two seniors headed to the Pac-12, as well as a junior who was in the top fifty of his class. No Nebraska school had ever faced a team ranked as high; Central found itself in the rare role of underdog, exactly what Behrens had sought.

After Central scored the first bucket of the third quarter, for a 26–19 lead, an upset and national affirmation was within its grasp. Then Poly went on a 25–9 run over the next eleven minutes for a 44–35 lead. Central clawed its way back, and Akoy's dunk tied it at 49 with just under a minute left. Poly worked for the last shot, and Central thought it had the ball when it went out of bounds with four seconds left. But Poly kept possession and inbounded to guard Ke'Jhan Feagin, who potted a 22-footer over the outstretched arm of Hollins, for a 52–49 final. Ouch.

"They're in tears, they're heartbroken," Behrens told the media. "They really fought and really wanted to win that game. That's how it should be. If it wasn't important it wouldn't hurt. It hurts because they cared. . . . I'm proud that they're hurt by a loss." Akoy tweeted: "I am so pissed off right now! Should have won tonight! Good job though guys!"

Both Central and Nebraska gained in stature with the narrow defeat. "Nebraska has some jewels," said Poly coach Sharrief Metoyer. "They have some guys who can play and they're catching up to the rest of the country." What Central did not gain, however, was the joy of an upset victory. It got another chance in its next game, in the loser's bracket against Whitney Young of Chicago. Whitney Young was an 1,800-student exam school whose alumni included First Lady Michelle Obama and NBA guard Quentin Richardson. The team was ranked No. 4 by MaxPreps and featured the top-ranked prospect for the class of 2014, Jahlil Okafor, a 6-foot-11, 260-pound center three years away from an NBA career.

Again Central was the underdog, and again it flirted with an upset victory, though it didn't look that way when Whitney Young took a nine-point lead early in the third quarter. But tough defense from Hollins and timely shooting from Thurman and Billingsley gave Central a 48–46 lead early in the fourth quarter. The lead seesawed until Whitney Young hit a 3 with 1:16 left for a 58–56 lead, then went up 60–57 and held on as Thurman and Hollins missed 3s in the final 30 seconds. Akoy had 14 points and 8 rebounds matched against Okafor, who had game highs of 23 points and 11 rebounds. "Akoy really held his own and opened some eyes," Behrens recalled.

Nonetheless, after winning forty straight in Nebraska, Central had lost two of three at City of Palms, though just barely. The narrow losses may have validated Central on a national stage, but they left a void where Behrens had hoped for joy. He summoned his inner Gene Hackman to rouse his players: "Guys, I will tell you something now, and I won't talk about it again until it comes up on the schedule," he said. "We're going to play Oak Hill later this year, and we're going to beat them. Count on it."

Four! **17**

Oak Hill Academy was Part 2 of Behrens's national experiment. Located at Mouth of Wilson, Virginia, Oak Hill was basketball royalty. Its 150 students paid about $33,000 a year to attend the Baptist-affiliated boarding school unless they could dribble, shoot, and rebound. Fifty-five D-1 scholarship players came out of Oak Hill between 2000 and 2012. Among its alumni with NBA pedigrees were Jerry Stackhouse, Carmelo Anthony, Kevin Durant, Rajon Rondo, Ty Lawson, Michael Beasley, Josh Smith, and Rod Strickland. In 2011–12 Oak Hill had gone 44-0 and had claimed its eighth mythical national championship in twenty years.

Central had fifteen games against local opponents before it got to Oak Hill, and for the first eleven of them things went as expected, which is to say that Central was methodical and victorious. Then the burden of expectations became too heavy, as Behrens had feared. In late January 2013, Central was upset at Papillion–La Vista, 67–58, for its first loss in Nebraska since February 18, 2011, a span of fifty-one games. As the clock ran out, La Vista's fans stormed the court in a show of exuberance usually reserved for state tournaments or films like *Hoosiers*. Central was back in its Muncie role and didn't like it one bit. "Yes, we lost, yes Papio deserved to win, yes we didn't play with heart until the end, yes everyone in the state is happy we lost," Akoy wrote. "But yes, we will win state in March!!!!"

The loss underscored the value of Hollins, who was out with a high ankle sprain. Central lost its next game to Omaha South, 65–59, again without Hollins in the lineup. Akoy wrote: "My Central Eagles we just got 2 regroup and become a team again like we were in the beginning! It's senior year! Go out with a bang!" Behrens recalled: "We were targets and they beat us. We had to regroup and refocus. When you lose, it hits you. Losing twice really hit us."

In the first week of February Hollins returned to the lineup, and Central won twice by wide margins. Those led up to February 9, when a caravan snaked west across I-80 to Grand Island, in the middle of the state, for the Heartland Hoops Classic and a showdown with Oak Hill. CHSF packed a bus with alumni, students and faculty car-pooled, and Lotte drove Adaw and some of Akoy's siblings. Nebraska fans were familiar with the "Big Game" vibe on football Saturdays at Memorial Stadium in Lincoln. A similar vibe enveloped Heartland Events Center. Most of the 5,500 spectators were local, which was to say white, and not apt to identify with the city school that started five blacks and dominated the division in which the local school struggled.

Central had arrived in late afternoon and had a walk-through at the arena to prepare for the 9 p.m. tip-off. Dinner, arranged by CHSF, was at a local country club. Unfortunately a chicken dish did not agree with Hollins and would come back, and up, to haunt him. When they returned to the arena, a game was in progress, and they were besieged for autographs. "First time I ever had that happen," recalled Tre'Shawn Thurman. "These kids came up to us, and I'm like, 'I'm in high school like you.' It was crazy. It felt like a college game."

During warm-ups Central finally got a look at an Oak Hill roster laden with talent destined for D-1 and beyond. Oak Hill featured 6-foot-6 Troy Williams (Indiana, Memphis Grizzlies), 6-foot-5 Sindarius Thornwell (South Carolina), 6-foot-1 Ike Iroegbu (Washington State), 6-foot-1 Nate Britt (North Carolina), 6-foot-5 R. J. Curington (DePaul), 5-foot-11 Terrence Phillips (Missouri), and 6-foot-8 Rokas Gustys (Hofstra). Though Oak Hill's 24-4 record had it ranked in the middle of most of the Top 25 polls, it was every bit as formidable as Long Beach Poly and Whitney Young, and it represented Central's last chance to beat a favored opponent. "There was a huge buzz," recalled Jay Landstrom. "I had never been to a big heavyweight fight in Las Vegas, but that's what it felt like."

Central senior Henry Hawbaker, a pal of Akoy's, got to the arena with classmates just before tip-off and could not find seats in the student section. "We had to sit in the Oak Hill section," Hawbaker recalled. "And then it hit me: how the heck does a high school in Virginia have a fan base that can travel to Nebraska? That got us really pumped." Tim Shipman was among a contingent of Central faculty members at the arena. "When Central got introduced, there was a noticeable anti-Central sentiment," Shipman recalled. "Those were the folks from out that way. A lot of people were just tired of Central being dominant."

In *Hoosiers* before the final game Hackman exhorts his players: "Five players on the floor function as one single unit. Team. Team. Team. No one player on the floor more important than the other." Behrens gave a talk with more specifics before the Oak Hill tip-off: "Share the ball, take good shots, get Akoy some touches. Transitional defense, get back, contain the ball, no dribble penetration, no easy baskets. Rebound on the defensive end."

The scoring opened with a slam-dunk by Akoy. Central sprinted to a 13–3 lead and led 17–14 after a quarter. The lead seesawed, with Oak Hill's biggest lead at 28–23 and Central ahead at the half, 33–32. Akoy had 10 points, while Hollins and K. J. Scott both had 8. Hollins's floor game was as fierce as usual, and it caught up to him in the locker room. "He puked for two minutes straight—everything he ate," recalled Jay Landstrom. "You could hear him in the stall."

Central came out strong in the third quarter, led by Akoy's three blocks, and harassed Oak Hill into 7 turnovers and 2-of-12 shooting. Then something unexpected and wonderful happened. "Akoy missed a dunk and put his jersey over his head at half court," Shipman recalled. "After that everybody started rooting for Central."

Behrens sensed the crowd shift too. "People from the middle of the state, from Grand Island, cheered for us," he recalled. "The script was flipped." Hawbaker, seated with Oak Hill fans, saw the change. "There were these Grand Island guys in leather jackets and trucker caps," he recalled. "They stood up and gave Akoy and Tra-Deon and K. J. a round of applause for representing the state. It was a great Nebraska moment."

Central led, 43–36, after three quarters, Oak Hill closed to within 49–47, but Thurman played through a sprained ankle to hit a couple of buckets, and Hollins and Hollins-Johnson nailed down the win with free throws. Final: Central 70, Oak Hill 63. Akoy led scorers with 20 points and grabbed 10 rebounds. The postgame locker room, Behrens recalled, was one of the most jubilant he'd ever seen. Afterward Central players, coaches, and family members lingered at the arena with fans and spectators and basked in their *Hoosiers* moment. "This was different than a regular-season win," Hollins told the media. "It was like we won state."

The *World-Herald*'s Stu Pospisil wrote, "Omaha Central gave the state a signature win for the ages. What else compares to the Eagles beating Oak Hill Academy, maybe the most recognizable name in high school basketball? Absolutely nothing." The Oak Hill victory brought pure joy to players and coaches. "It gave us a chance to win a game people didn't think we could win," Behrens recalled. "It was good mentally to win and feel that exhilaration."

For one magical night Central got to be Milan and David and all the underdogs of legend and myth. The experience proved to be as therapeutic and energizing as Behrens had hoped. Over the next four weeks Central fashioned one of the most dominant runs in Nebraska hoops history. It won two games left in the regular season by 31 points and 61 points. In the districts it dispatched Grand Island, 70–35, and then Omaha Burke, 66–51. On Tuesday before the state tournament Behrens kicked Akoy out of practice, the cause of which has been lost in time. What it meant was that Central was primed and ready. "As a coach I was wired and locked in," Behrens recalled. "I probably kicked him out to send a message."

At state, Papillion–LaVista South was toppled, 61–41, and Omaha Benson went down, 80–50, in the semifinal. The final matched Central against Papillion–La Vista, to whom it had lost in January and for whom it nursed a bit of a grudge because its crowd had rushed the court. Behrens was superstitious enough to wear the same blue shirt and tie he had worn for his previous six finals, and before tip-off he indulged himself one more Gene Hackman moment, even though his team was favored: "Forget about legacies and history," he told his players. "Think of this like a pickup game at the Y. Just do your thing." To his seven seniors he said, "Play your best game in your last game."

At center court, as Akoy readied for tip-off, he slowed the moment and scanned the sold-out Devaney Center. He was on the verge of an unprecedented achievement in Nebraska high school basketball—his fourth Class A championship. Close by were his teammates and coaches, the guys he huddled with before each game, fists raised, and chanted, "One, Two, Three, Family." He would miss this group, this band of brothers, though he would not miss being run like a dog and kicked out of practice by Behrens.

Beyond was the student section, the kids who shared the classrooms and hallways of Nebraska's oldest high school and who now were in full roar. There were his teachers, even the ones who didn't like basketball but attended as a show of support, and there were the administrators, for whom he cheerfully served as "ambassador" of Central. His high school was special, he was sure of it, a downtown melting pot that had survived fickle economics and politics and endured wave upon wave of nostalgic alumni.

There was Scott Hammer, svengali of his grassroots "select" teams, summer camps, air travel, and hotel rooms—his world apart from high school. There were Dave and Ann Sjulin, salt of the earth, who embraced him as a virtual son-in-law. Akoy's gaze settled on their daughter, Lotte, and for maybe the millionth time he contemplated her fresh athletic beauty. He considered the Hammers and Sjulins his adoptive families, even though their pigmentations and backgrounds were as different from his as night and day. Thank heavens their refrigerators were as open and welcoming as they were.

There were the media he had courted and cultivated to mutual satisfaction. And there, arrayed around the court, were the photographers to whom he would grant one last iconic image to remember him by.

Then his eyes came upon the object of his deepest affection and concern: Adaw Makier, his mother. She had come to Lincoln in his honor, to watch a game she barely comprehended. He thought about the miracle of her presence at his final high school game. She had gotten out of Sudan with little more than the clothes on her back, fourteen years earlier, a refugee of a violent civil war that had killed hundreds of thousands. She had gotten him out too; he owed her his life. Then too he owed his father, Madut Agau, who was not among the familiar faces this day because he worked at a meat plant on weekends for time-and-a-half. His family had limped ashore in Omaha, at the mercy of strangers, and had found both hardship and generosity. Each day was a lesson in a new culture and a reminder of the old. Now he felt responsible for his parents and five (soon to be six) younger siblings. This game was as much for them as for him; they were his duty, and they were his dilemma.

Akoy Agau was about to jump tip-off to the Nebraska Class A basketball championship, another step in his remarkable journey out of Africa. Where it led he knew not, but on this day, in this moment, he would play the game he loved to fulfill a prophecy and make history.

Behrens had exhorted the seniors, and they complied. Their last game, indeed, would be their best. Akoy had 6 blocks in the first quarter on the way to a 33–12 lead midway through the second quarter. Hollins clamped down on La Vista's top scorer and held him to 7 points. The Eagles stole the ball, pounded the boards, and ran the floor. Behind-the-back passes led to alley-oop dunks. It was "the closest thing to the Harlem Globetrotters we'll see in high school basketball," wrote Dirk Chatelain of the *World-Herald*. Tempers flared after a frustrated defender upended Hollins, but no punches were thrown. With nearly three minutes left Behrens pulled his starters and let his reserves finish the 69–44 blowout. As the clock ran down, Hollins hectored Behrens on the bench, "You should have put me on varsity as a freshman."

That was it. Akoy's "Four" arrived with a flourish though with little suspense. His stat line of 8 points, 5 rebounds, and 8 blocked shots was modest compared to his past finals. Nor did his season averages of 12.8 points and 6.1 rebounds, along with 81 blocked shots, leap off the stat sheet. In Behrens's system the only stat that mattered was Central's record 75-point margin of victory for the three tournament games combined. Akoy mounted a ladder and cut down a net with a joyous flourish. As the team awaited the presentation ceremony, he heard his name called from Central's student section near the team bench. The Central kids were stoked.

"He looked over at us with a goofy grin," recalled Henry Hawbaker. Akoy feigned a step toward the student section.

"Come on over," somebody yelled. Drama. Akoy could not resist. He made a move toward his schoolmates.

"Run Akoy!" He got up to speed in a few strides. Hawbaker and senior Tyler Miles and a few others joined shoulders and braced. Then Akoy launched himself. "He was 230 pounds, and we caught him," Hawbaker recalled. "Everyone in the student section went nuts."

A *World-Herald* photographer captured the image: Akoy in full roar with part of a net around his neck, held aloft by Hawbaker and Miles, in a sea of jubilant students. If some pictures are worth a thousand words, this one was worth a million. Its narrative, of acceptance and accomplishment, was Akoy's journey from African refugee to American citizen.

A short time later, when the trophy and medals were presented and his teammates danced and shouted, Akoy crouched down, pulled his shirt over his face, and cried. He later explained, "It was sad; it was happy; it was all the emotions mixed together."

The photo of Akoy held aloft by Hawbaker and Miles ran the next day above the caption: "Nebraska's Head of State."

Spring Prom   **18**

Spring was a whirl for Akoy as Nebraska's unelected head of state. Nebraska's elected head of state, Gov. Dave Heineman, declared March 18, 2013, as Omaha Central Eagles Basketball Day. At the state capitol Heineman presented Behrens a plaque, with Akoy at his side and the team in front of a huge American flag. Heineman's proclamation, in part, read, "The Omaha Central players and community are to be recognized for their outstanding achievements and accomplishments as they go on to even bigger and brighter futures." As players and coaches walked through the capitol halls, senators and staff members congratulated them and asked for pictures.

The next day Akoy flew to Haiti, with Lotte and Ann, on a "mission" to help an orphanage. He had volunteered when a berth came open on the trip organized by a teacher at Lotte's school. Ann offered medical service, while Lotte, Akoy, and the others played games with the children and cleaned and painted the orphanage. An eighteen-year-old orphan was about to move out, Akoy recalled, and "we helped finish up a house for him." At the end of their stay they left behind all clothes and shoes except what they wore, in what was a charitable gesture by the teenagers from west Omaha, whose closets overflowed, and something more by Akoy, whose closet did not.

Back in Omaha Akoy appeared in a "Harlem Shake" video, produced by the *World-Herald*, with the ten boys and girls first-team All-State selections, which included Hollins, augmented by students, band members, cheerleaders, and mascots. In it Akoy wore his purple Central uniform and danced Gangnam Style, ever compatible with a camera lens. Then he returned to the state capitol and was introduced to the legislature as part of the *Lincoln Journal Star* Super-State team. As the newspaper reported, he "leaned over the balcony ledge to wave to senators and just generally hammed it up. . . . In the Rotunda, he stepped up to a podium in place for an upcoming press conference to 'address' the assembled group." By the end of March Akoy was back on Twitter, which he had sacrificed for Lent—except now he posted less often and revealed less as he became more discreet about his public image, in accord with Pitino's policy at Louisville.

A certain type of stage and publicity, however, Akoy found irresistible. The Central spring prom loomed on the schedule. Akoy wanted to double date with Lotte and another couple, Henry Hawbaker and Lauren Wegner. But Akoy and Hawbaker had procrastinated, and time was short. They were halfway in the doghouse and needed a reprieve. "We need to do something big," Akoy said.

"Big," Akoy decided, was televised coverage of their prom invitations. "Now, Akoy makes claims one wouldn't find realistic all the time," Hawbaker recalled. "I thought he was bullshitting me. How the heck was he going to make this happen?"

It turned out that Akoy was friendly with Thor Tripp, a sportscaster for KETV 7, the ABC affiliate. "We had a pretty good relationship, to where he felt comfortable asking me," Tripp recalled. "Normally a TV station wouldn't do something like that, but we had done so much with him, and he was so well known locally, regardless of whether it was normal or not, it was good TV."

Tripp had been at the station for two years and had come to appreciate Akoy's camera presence at live events. "If I was shooting, he would come to the camera and act like it was a mirror," Tripp recalled. "Walking on the court he would chant something or have words for his teammates. He knew how to play to the camera."

With Tripp a go, Akoy and Hawbaker brainstormed a script. Lotte and Lauren played select softball; why not create a softball scene? So on an afternoon in early April they met Tripp at Elmwood Park, in athletic shorts and T-shirts, and found a dirt infield and backstop. Hawbaker had a bat, gloves, and softballs; Tripp had a camera; and Akoy had himself.

First they scrawled "PROM?" in large capital letters with a question mark on the infield dirt. Akoy stood on the mound, Hawbaker in the batter's box. Tripp, as the shooter, captured the action. Akoy lobbed an underhand pitch to Hawbaker, who swatted it to the outfield. Akoy turned, in mock disgust, and watched the flight.

Next Tripp shot Akoy and Hawbaker in the infield as they walked toward the camera. "Now, we may not be as good at softball as you guys are," said Hawbaker. "But the way we see it, you guys only have one option," said Akoy. At that Akoy tossed the glove. It landed in the dirt, next to the bat, under the inscription of "PROM?"

Separately Hawbaker said, "Lauren Wegner," and Akoy said, "Charlotte Sjulin," and in unison they said, "Will you go to prom with us?"

Akoy looked at Hawbaker. "You think they'll say yes?"

"I hope they'll say yes."

"Please say yes."

The scene ended with Akoy's and Hawbaker's hands cupped in mock prayer. The shoot took about forty-five minutes, which Tripp edited to a fifty-second segment and set to Queen's "We Will Rock You." It aired on a Sunday evening newscast, which Akoy and Lotte watched at her house and Hawbaker and Wegner watched at Wegner's house. Both girls accepted the invitations, and Lotte posted to Akoy's Twitter feed, "I guess @heyheyhawbaker and @ZerotheHeroAkoy did an alright job of asking @ralphlauren_w and me to prom!"

Next morning the prom invite was the buzz at Central. "Talk about a good Monday," Hawbaker recalled. "All the teachers saw it, and all the kids heard about it. Half of the school high-fived us, and the other half gave us shit."

Akoy's celebrity elevated another level, to where autograph requests were commonplace. Early in April he attended the two-day FBLA convention in Omaha at the Ramada Inn on South Seventy-Second Street. When he entered the lobby, students crowded him. "A girl ran up to him like she had seen Michael Jackson," recalled Denise Powers, faculty adviser. "She squealed, 'O, my God, I can't believe this; I have to get a picture with you; my boyfriend is going to die.' It was like we had a movie star with us."

As always, with Akoy the question was not whether attention would go to his head but how. Powers found out the next evening when Akoy left the motel with a few friends to play video games. "The one rule is you have to be back at curfew," Powers recalled. "That's my responsibility and my liability. That night he was late and didn't answer his phone. I kept asking Lotte, and she didn't know; he didn't answer her either. Her school didn't have rooms at the hotel, so she went home.

"I waited and waited, and finally he came back. I chewed him out; I was so worried something had happened to him. I talked to him about respect and follow-through. I told him I was hurt he didn't communicate with me; every student knows how to pick up a phone. I was so worried I cried and said, 'Don't you ever do this again.' He apologized for his behavior and gave me a hug and said it would never happen again."

To Akoy's credit, Powers recalled, he participated in the next day's events as though nothing had happened. At dinner, when Powers was late to the banquet room, Akoy gave up his seat so she could eat with her students. "He went to a random table and asked if he could sit with them," Powers recalled. "He was caring."

In the hallways of Central Akoy exuded humility. A star-struck freshman, Jacob Bigelow, walked past him and shouted a greeting. "He stopped and asked me my name," Bigelow recalled. "He said he was glad to meet me." If he felt otherwise, nobody was sure. Akoy could be as opaque and smooth as a politician. "He's got the same look on his face at all times," Tra-Deon Hollins told a reporter. "You wouldn't know that he's mad at you unless he tells you." Said Behrens: "He knows how to work whatever room he's in. He knows how to talk to his seventeen-year-old friends and how to talk to the boardroom full of adults."

Akoy penned an essay for the *Louisville Courier-Journal* in which he predicted Louisville would win the Final Four, which it did. He wrote of Pitino, "The things that Coach P has done over the years are tremendous. He is at times said to be crazy, but I think I'm ready." And he wrote of himself, "I have done all I could in high school, and now it's on to college. I call it the journey to being like Bill Russell. I have one more state championship than he does, so that's a good start."

Akoy traveled to Louisville to play in the Kentucky Derby Festival Basketball Classic. Back in Omaha he won an award for outstanding male academic athlete given annually at the B'nai B'rith Sports Banquet. The award, after his early struggles in school, defined him in a way that sports-only awards could not.

The 2013 *O-Book*, volume 116, was published. It featured tattoos and body piercings of students and a poll that ranked Rihanna as favorite artist and Kanye West's "Mercy" and Taylor Swift's "We Are Never Ever Getting Back Together" among top songs. It saluted "Champ High's Dynasty" and offered a reflection from Akoy: "Goals are set before dreams are made. I had the goal and dream to win four straight state championships and I've done just that. Now I'm setting goals and dreams for college."

May was filled with graduation events. On the last day of May Akoy packed his bags and sent out the final tweet of his high school career. "It's been great Omaha, NE. Time to move on to the next chapter of my life. I'm on my way to my Louisville Cardinals!!! L1c4!!!"

Akoy's college career began with a tweet on June 1: "Flat Tire on the way to Louisville! Terrible way to start!!!"

He made it to Louisville for a few days of orientation and while there opened an Instagram account. In August, back in Omaha, he dropped by Central, in summer recess, and ambled through the quiet halls. He poked his head into the principal's office and saw that it was empty. Then he settled into the big chair behind the desk and propped his size 16s atop it. They were on ample display when in walked Edward Bennett, who had been named the new principal upon Bigsby's retirement in June.

Bennett cleared his throat. "Hello, sir," Akoy said. "I came back to see if things were okay."

Years later Bennett remembered the moment. "I felt honored," he recalled. "Akoy was Akoy. He hadn't forgotten about us."

Repatriation 19

To return or not was the question a South Sudanese refugee could not avoid. Repatriation was as personal as it was perilous.

A much-admired naturalized Nebraskan, Lam Chuol Thichuong, was among those who returned. He had come out of a refugee camp in Ethiopia, resettled from Minnesota to Omaha in 1998, worked as bilingual liaison for the Omaha schools, and earned a degree at UNO. Sworn in as a U.S. citizen ten days after the 9/11 attacks, he enlisted in the Marine Corps and served a tour of duty in Iraq. After his tour he returned to Omaha, worked at the Charles Drew Health Center, served on the board of the South Sudan Community Association, and helped his wife raise two daughters. But his homeland called to him, and with the help of an Omaha connection, Miyong Kuon, Thichuong landed a job as personal aide and secretary to autonomous South Sudanese vice-president Riek Machar in 2007. Then civil war erupted, pitting the Nuer-based opposition of Machar against the Dinka-based government of Salva Kiir. When shooting began on the night of December 15, 2013, President Kiir's soldiers gunned down Thichuong, thirty-nine, and his brother Pal in the streets of Juba.

Among the Nuer partisans was Miyong Kuon, who in the early 2000s had worked as an ESL paraprofessional at Central while he raised his younger twin brothers. As an undergraduate in journalism at UNO, Kuon had interviewed Machar. When the 2005 peace deal granted autonomy and an option for independence to South Sudan and Machar became vice-president, he hired Kuon as a communications aide. From then on Kuon split his time between Omaha and South Sudan. Six months after the vote for independence in 2011, Kuon stood outside the United Nations in New York with the delegation from South Sudan as it hoisted its new flag for the first time. In 2012 Kuon and Thichuong arranged for Machar's first visit to Omaha. After civil war broke out in 2013 and Machar fled to Kenya, Kuon followed him. Subsequently he shuttled among Addis Ababa, Ethiopia, the site of peace talks; New York, where he represented Machar's followers at the United Nations; and Omaha, to be with his wife and five children.

In 2015 Kuon had arranged for Machar's second visit to Omaha. For help he turned to an old friend, Lol Kuek (Central 2002), who had changed his name to Changkuoth Gatkuoth while a student at UNO. Changkuoth, which means "Sunday" in Nuer, had been his given name in Sudan, and Gatkuoth was his late father's name. He worked as a microbiology lab technician for Hormel Foods in Minnesota and had a wife and four children. Yet his belief in Machar's cause was such that he returned to Omaha to help organize his visit. Later he posted a video in which he described the Dinka as "imperialists" who are compelled to subjugate the Nuer.

Gatkuoth mulled a return to South Sudan to join a friend and fellow Central graduate, Gatong Gatluak (2000), who had been a member of the South Sudan parliament. After civil war erupted, Gatluak joined the army of Machar, near the Ethiopian border, and was promoted to the rank of general. "Many of my friends went back to South Sudan to be soldiers, and they want me back there as well," Gatkuoth said. "I have little kids to take care of, but I'm definitely thinking about it. I'd rather be part of it and do what I can to fix it."

A plea for unity and peace came from NBA star Luol Deng, who brought his second South Sudan Unite festival to Omaha for three days in 2016. "This event is about unity, it's about us coming together and sharing positive energy and helping each other," said Deng in a public statement. Deng acknowledged a "lot of negative energy and negative news" about his event. Some of the Nuer in Omaha blamed the violence in South Sudan on his father's political organization, the Dinka Council of Elders, alleged to exacerbate tribal divisions. Deng said that the festival was not about politics, tribes, or money. "I know there's a lot of hurt and pain," he said, "but by us coming together we can really work on a better future for South Sudan and all of us."

Civil war escalated, and more refugees fled. "The new arrivals in Uganda are reporting ongoing fighting as well as looting by armed militias, burning down of homes, and murders of civilians," UNHCR reported. The humanitarian organization Doctors without Borders reported from its clinic in Juba that the injured "included children as young as two years old who had been shot when armed men broke into their homes." Famine and cholera deepened the misery in South Sudan. An estimated 50,000 had died in the conflict, while 1.69 million people were displaced internally, and 831,582 had fled to Ethiopia, Sudan, and Uganda, the UNHCR reported in July 2016.

In late summer 2016 Akoy took me to Mason School Apartments, where he had lived his first six and a half years in Omaha. He guided me through the hallways and pointed out the stairwells and vestibules of his youth. He peered through a door that faced a parking lot to the west. "Fourth of July fireworks out there," he recalled. "The kind you launched at one another. I loved the Fourth."

Akoy ran into a young South Sudanese woman he greeted with a hug. Nancy Peter had been his neighbor at the Mason and was still a resident with her mother, Bernadita. Like Akoy, Nancy Peter was born in Khartoum and had fled to Egypt at a young age. She came to Omaha in 2004 as a nine-year-old, and within a year she and her mother had moved into the Mason. She was close to Akoy's age, but because he hung out with the older south Sudanese boys, she had kept her distance. "It was frowned upon for girls to hang out with guys if you were younger," Nancy recalled. She made friends with Akoy's younger brother, Maguy, and spent many happy evenings at the Agau apartment, sharing in Adaw's spaghetti dinners. After Akoy's family moved from the Mason, she had not watched Akoy play basketball, although she was well aware of his celebrity. "All the little kids in Omaha looked up to him, especially the Sudanese," Nancy recalled.

Nancy invited us into her first-floor apartment, where Akoy hugged Bernadita, who wore traditional African garb. We were beckoned to sit and were offered tea and water. Nancy talked about how most of the South Sudanese had left the Mason and that residents were predominantly African American and white. The walls of the hallways, which had featured colorful African mosaics, had been painted over by new management. "My guess is they wanted to cover up the tribal stuff to appeal to non-Africans," Nancy said. Akoy and Nancy updated one another on school. Nancy was at UNO in pre-med with an eye toward pediatrics. Akoy had switched his major from pre-med to anthropology and English. "Thinking about the law," he said.

Conversation commenced between Akoy and Bernadita in Arabic. Bernadita wanted me to know that Akoy and Nancy were "good kids" who brought honor to their parents, according to the translation Akoy provided. They talked about South Sudan's ongoing civil war. The fighting in South Sudan had to stop, Akoy and Bernadita both agreed, and the United States should intercede to negotiate a truce. Bernadita liked President Obama, but she hoped the next president would do more for South Sudan. The South Sudanese had so many needs, from schools to hospitals to utilities to basic necessities like shoes. "It's important to help the people in South Sudan," Bernadita said.

Talk came around to repatriation, as often it did among South Sudanese refugees. For young Sudanese Americans who were born in Sudan, such as Akoy and Nancy, repatriation was both an act of conscience and an affirmation of progressive American values. Nancy had gone back to Juba, South Sudan, in 2015 to visit her father, who worked for the United Nations in transportation. He had once lived in the United States, but his green card had expired, and he could not return. "I liked being there because everyone was African, and they weren't denying where they were from," Nancy said. "I felt more at home." Nancy said she wanted to work in South Sudan as a doctor, for the United Nations or for Doctors without Borders. Akoy nodded as if he had thought at length about repatriation. "I've always wanted to go back home," he said. "I want to help, if basketball works out." He cited Dikembe Mutombo, from the Democratic Republic of Congo, who had become an NBA Hall of Famer. "A lot of players like him are active in going back to their country, taking money to have things built, being vocal for the community. That's what I want to do. If I play pro ball, there are benefits that come with that. I would love to go back and see where I was as a kid."

Not much was left to say. Akoy hugged his hosts again, promised to stay in touch, and lost himself in thought as we left the Mason. He had been so courteous and gentlemanly with Nancy and Bernadita that he connected himself, unknowingly, to a thread of Mason mythology. It had been related to me by Mabel Boyd, who had worked at the Mason School as a secretary, and by Raydelle Meehan, who had taught at the school in the 1970s.

Legend has it that a little boy named Frederic Austerlitz attended or visited the Mason School after the turn of the century. When he was six or seven, Austerlitz moved to New York City with his sister and mother and launched an entertainment career. He took the stage name of Fred Astaire and became America's most iconic song-and-dance performer, smooth and urbane and polished, the embodiment of suave. If you're a baby boomer like me, you know because your parents were his fans. If you're younger and you don't, go to YouTube and watch "Fred Astaire and Rita Hayworth—Amazing dance scene."

Omaha records show that young Austerlitz, born in 1899, attended the Paul Street School, now known as Kellom School, in north Omaha. But Boyd and Meehan believed that Austerlitz may have attended the Mason for a short time, or at the very least visited it on a return to Omaha, and perhaps performed an impromptu dance. They believed the archived records of the Mason School, boxed in a South Omaha basement, would bear them out.

I wanted to believe the legend for the lovely karma it created. If it was true, then Akoy, as a boy in the Mason Street Apartments, ran the hallways where Fred Astaire's feet had skipped and danced a hundred years before. As he grew in size and stature and rose to the top of Nebraska schoolboy basketball, Akoy channeled Astaire in his elegance and panache. Had he played in top hat and tails, he would have been perfectly at ease. The same was true off the court.

That a South Sudanese refugee could fashion himself as an American ideal said a lot about Akoy and something about America. The debate about who should get in and who should not has gone on for most of our history and no doubt will continue. The beauty of America is that whoever gets in can be like Fred Astaire. Or not. They can return to their native land. Or not.

Getting It Right   **20**

The South Sudanese diaspora displaced thousands of refugees to the land down under, where basketball was embraced with a passion. In Australia the first South Sudanese National Basketball tournament was held in 2003 with four teams. Basketball, said organizer Manyang G. Berberi, not only served health and recreation, it helped refugees integrate into mainstream culture. In 2009 team managers throughout the country formed the South Sudanese Australian National Basketball Association. By 2017 the South Sudanese Australian National Classic—as the tournament came to be known—featured more than fifty teams and six hundred players.

A club in Blacktown, a western suburb of Sydney, sprang up in 2006 to nurture South Sudanese refugees. Called Savannah Pride, the club's stated mission is to provide "well-rounded development for boys and girls with basketball programs, education programs, homework support and cultural guidance." Within a couple of years it began to funnel its best players to private high schools and colleges in the United States and Canada. One of those players, 7-foot-1 Thon Maker, was the top draft pick of the Milwaukee Bucks in 2016. America had no counterpart to the Australian association, but South Sudanese American hoopsters thrived nonetheless. When Akoy left high school in 2013, up to thirty had played or were playing for American colleges.

The Omaha Talons formed in 2012 in the mold of Savannah Pride. Conceived and run by Koang Doluony, the first South Sudanese player to make a name in Nebraska, the Talons sought to empower the South Sudanese community. Doluony had played at Indiana State and UNO, gotten a degree in criminology, and started the Talons to engage South Sudanese youth in personal growth and economic uplift. The club also gave him a podium. At twenty-six he was a serious and articulate student of history and politics with concerns about the South Sudanese diaspora and South Sudan.

On a sultry late August evening about thirty of the Talons, most of South Sudanese descent, drilled and scrimmaged at an indoor gym in north Omaha. Akoy was on hand to help Doluony and his assistant, longtime friend Ty Gatuoch. There were drills for the younger players, Akoy's eight-year-old brother Akol among them, and there were scrimmages for players from the mid-teens to early twenties. The Talons counted up to 150 youth for their big events, many drawn to basketball by Akoy's success. While the Talons practiced, Doluony found a quiet stairwell away from the action and told me what was on his mind, which was a lot.

"A kid this morning missed his bus to school, thirty minutes from school," Doluony said. "I had to go pick him up, so as I'm driving him to school, he tells me he had three workouts the day before, and he's had nothing but ramen noodles in his stomach for the last two days. His mom isn't able to go grocery shopping or take him to school because she failed her license test because she doesn't speak English and can't go to the DMV and have a way of passing the written test, and there's no system in place that can help her meet those standards. This kid is in school all day, and he's playing a game at 7 p.m., and the only thing he'll have in his stomach is the school lunch, which doesn't even feel like food when you eat it, but that's all he'll have to eat. He will stay after school until that game, and he won't get home until 10 p.m. His parents won't be at his game even though the other parents are."

There was frustration in his voice as Doluony described the struggle of the South Sudanese diaspora. The school system, for instance, provided only one teacher who spoke Nuer, the most common South Sudanese dialect in Omaha. Resettlement services were inadequate, he said: "The city should be taking time to mentor our mothers and fathers, helping us understand housing, employment, business startups, voting rights, and the political process. To this day we feel segregated. . . . I know it's not just the South Sudanese community, but it's every community in Omaha where everybody pretty much is on their own."

The struggle was internal too. In Africa, Doluony said, the South Sudanese "interpreted the world through our feelings in an intuitive culture,"
which sprang from minimal government and possessions. America was
about logic and institutions and material wealth. "In order for me to really
survive I have to leave the Sudanese aspect at home and get my brain to
where I can logically navigate things I have to do. I have to pursue money
and figure out a way to materially keep up."

Doluony offered up his own bittersweet journey to explain the challenges
of assimilation. His father was a pastor who at one time oversaw four
Christian churches in the Upper Nile region of south Sudan. In 1986 his
family moved to Ethiopia, where for the next thirteen years they lived in
two refugee camps. Koang was born in 1990, the fourth of seven children,
in Dema, Ethiopia. In 1999 the family was admitted to the United States
and was resettled in Rochester, New York, which proved to be hospitable,
except that it lacked a south Sudanese community, and Doluony's mother
felt isolated. So in 2000 the family moved to Omaha. "Part of my mother's
desire to move was to have peers, other women, to be with," Doluony said.

The move didn't work out for Doluony's oldest brother, Kueth, who had
been a math prodigy as a high school sophomore and had interned for a
professor at the Rochester Institute of Technology. As a junior at Omaha
Central he felt lost. "Soon as he got into Central, they stuck him in an
ESL class and expectations went downhill," Doluony recalled. "Nobody
took the time to understand that this kid might be special. So instead of
academics being his focus, he decided he had to work to help the family.
He got a couple of jobs." Kueth enlisted after high school, served in Iraq,
and sent money home so that the family could have cable television and
cell phones. At thirty-five, married and a father, Kueth was depressed.
"When you're not able to be all you can be, a part of you dies," Doluony
said. "He feels like he didn't pan out to be what he could be, and a lot of
that was because he put personal ambition aside for me and my siblings."

In 2002 Doluony's father became the first south Sudanese licensed as
a Baptist minister in Nebraska. His pulpit was at South Omaha's Bethel
Missionary Baptist Church, traditionally attended by African Americans—

Central High basketball legend Dwaine Dillard had sung in its choir as a child in the 1950s—and where African Americans and south Sudanese refugees struggled to find common ground. Close by Bethel Baptist were the Southside Terrace Apartments, subsidized housing where the Doluonys and Adaw's sister Teresa and her family lived.

Doluony's father was a better preacher than provider, so his mother worked at the Tyson meat plant, where Akoy's father worked, to support her children. Doluony remembered her coming home late at night, shoulders sore from cutting meat in a refrigerated room for eight or nine hours. "She wore three different coats and sweatshirts to go to work," Doluony recalled. "She was sick periodically from cutting meat." Half of her paycheck went back to her family in south Sudan, and the rest to the household budget. "My siblings and I each got one set of clothes and a pair of shoes, once a year, for school," he said. "That was my outfit; the rest of my clothes were hand-me-downs or from the Open Door Mission. A lot of times I would come home and dinner was a glass of milk, and if we had sugar around, that's what we would eat. Or frozen pizza. My mother was never around to cook." Eventually Doluony's mother got hired at First Data, where she was warm but still worked manual labor.

Doluony was eleven when he discovered the outdoor court at Southgate Apartments in Bellevue, three miles south of his home. Southgate was the south Sudanese version of Rucker Park, the legendary hoops crucible in Harlem. "Those were the first generation immigrants," Doluony recalled. "The level of talent was so high that to this day, even at D-1, I haven't met better athletes. I grew up playing against those guys and fell in love with the game. They played at such a high level, they made me successful in high school and gave me a chance to go to college."

Doluony's D-1 scholarship was a triumph for his family and for the South Sudanese outdoor courts—Southgate and Pulaski Park—where he built his game. Only later did he understand how the athletes on those courts, like his older brother, had sacrificed. "Those guys, most of them, had come on their own, not with their families," he recalled. "So they didn't have the luxury of playing high school basketball. They could do it as a recreation but not as something to invest themselves in. The unfortunate thing about those guys is even though they were school age, they couldn't be children. They had to grow up not only to raise themselves here but to support the families they left behind in Sudan."

When Doluony recalled the lost potential of those athletes, and of his brother, he worried about Akoy. "Being the oldest kid in a South Sudanese family means he's always had to be responsible for family, not just himself," he said. "Akoy always was forced to grow well beyond his years, and that hurts you. His challenge is to understand the best way he can take care of his family is by taking care of himself. By committing to the day-to-day process of what he has to do to be a successful student and athlete. His challenge is how does he put himself in a position where instead of focusing on what his mom needs or little brothers need, how does he lock in on being a student and athlete so that in the years after college he can truly help out his family?"

South Sudanese youth, like Akoy, needed to find a balance between assimilation and cultural preservation. This was tricky, Doluony conceded, because some cultural roots were best forgotten, and some models of assimilation were best avoided. These nuances were particularly subtle for South Sudanese girls. "Our culture has a very reserved ideology and mindset toward women," he said. "Certain processes have to happen for somebody to be heard."

Doluony recounted the experience of his older sister, Nyajuok, who went by the name of Rebecca. When the Doluonys came to Omaha in 2000, she enrolled at Central High as a fifteen-year-old sophomore. She was a good student, but her father was bound by tradition and arranged for her to marry an older south Sudanese man in exchange for cash, rather than cows, as was customary in south Sudan. Nebraska law allowed marriage at the age of nineteen or with parental consent at seventeen. Iowa allowed marriage at sixteen, and Missouri allowed marriage at fifteen with parental consent. Although marriage of underage south Sudanese girls was not commonplace and occurred beneath the radar of Omaha authorities, community leaders had held a meeting in 1999 to discourage it. Girls were said to have some choice in the matter, though they had little power in traditional south Sudanese culture. "My sister knew the only way out of it was to have a baby," Doluony recalled. "She went and got pregnant by a guy she was dating but who she knew she wouldn't stay with. She had the baby and got kicked out of the house." On her own Rebecca raised her little girl, graduated from Northwest High, got a nursing degree, and enlisted in the army. "The level of sacrifice she made, I would call my sister extraordinary," Doluony said. Stationed at Fort Campbell, Rebecca rose to the rank of captain, married, and gave birth to a son.

Young South Sudanese women needed to be empowered both within their families, which tended to be protective and domineering, and by the mainstream culture to which they aspired. "The American standard of beauty does not reflect on them in any way from the time they're in school and want to feel beautiful and liked and appreciated," Doluony said. "The standard of beauty here is something they can never seem to fit, and that breaks them. A lot of women in our community are bleaching their skin. They put cream on themselves to be lighter so that maybe they can attract guys they're attracted to. You have girls investing hundreds of dollars in hair extensions so they can be considered beautiful. So that instead of attracting a man that's going to love you for who you are, you mold yourself into what you think men like. Now instead of finding love, you're with guys who only want you because of x, y, and z."

South Sudanese males also struggled to find a constructive model for assimilation. Many had gravitated toward African American hip-hop culture in the early 2000s, which Doluony believed led to the rise of South Sudanese street gangs later in the decade, with negative effect on South Sudanese girls and women. "A lot of these young men, because of hip-hop, don't know how to show affection to their sisters, don't know how to talk to the Sudanese girls they date, don't know how to express to their moms how much they love them," he said, "That's not part of our culture. Our culture is to nurture and care for our sisters and girlfriends and let our moms know how much they mean to us."

The Talons wanted to help first- and second-generation South Sudanese find a balance. "We have the cultural challenges of how do you assimilate, and what is the right culture to assimilate to," said Doluony. "Do we become a product of our environment, African American urban America, or do we take the time to understand suburban west Omaha and the American Dream? What we have in front of us is like a blank sheet. We can rewrite the story of who we are and who we're becoming."

The stakes were high, as Doluony came to realize on Riek Machar's second visit to Omaha in October 2015. The exiled vice-president of South Sudan, leader of the Nuer faction in the ongoing civil war, was on tour to rally support. Among the expatriates he met was Doluony, who told him about the Talons. "I am impressed by what I have heard from these young people," Machar said. "They should live their lives here, make the opportunities. Some will be scientists, some will be basketballers, some will be entrepreneurs." Machar said that the young South Sudanese who grow up in Omaha, and throughout America, will teach South Sudan about democracy, set an example, and serve as an important bridge with the United States.

Machar's visit deepened Doluony's purpose. He told me: "Omaha is that one place where, if we do not get it right here, if we do not figure out a way for this community to have a comfortable identity, and if we're not growing the way we need to as a community, it's going to have a lot of implications all the way back to South Sudan. If we do get it right, and we do become a successful part of America, and you see South Sudanese representatives in government positions in a few years, it's going to have positive implications in South Sudan. The challenge is how do we get Omaha, not just the Sudanese but the entire city, to see that? And how do we put ourselves in a position where we can be a player?"

"How do you do that?" I asked.

The Talons would expand their programming, he said, as funding permitted. Money was a problem; they needed institutional and public support. He planned to get certified as a deputy registrar to organize the

South Sudanese vote into a potent bloc in local politics. In the meantime, each and every South Sudanese with a public profile had a responsibility to speak out.

"Basketball is the only thing that's given us a chance to have a voice," Doluony said. "And basketball players like me and Akoy, we're the only ones being accepted. The responsibility we have is being bigger than ourselves. If Akoy is in a position, when he speaks, where people are willing to listen and are interested in being a part of his life, it's his responsibility to be a voice for us, to truly represent us."

Beyond

21

The flat tire Akoy tweeted about on the road to Louisville foreshadowed Act Two. He saw limited action as a freshman. His conditioning was not up to Rick Pitino's standards, and two months into the season he was suspended one game by Pitino for an "attitude" issue. He underwent surgery for a sports hernia before his sophomore season, and he saw even less action. Impatient, he transferred after his third semester, a decision he later regretted as impulsive.

Akoy was open to Nebraska, but the Cornhuskers showed little interest, so he signed on with Georgetown. He expected to play, until he tore a knee ligament, which ended what would have been his third season before it began. Akoy wrote of his struggle and faith a few days before Christmas 2015 on an Instagram (gmb_ak47) post: "Sometimes I stay up at night thinking of everyone who started with me from the beginning . . . doing well and getting to shine. Everything is going the way they planned. I'm happy for them, but it's also frustrating. While my whole college career has been full of injuries and I haven't come close to achieving anything I wanted to. I'm just wondering when my time is coming. . . . Then I remember. . . . Everything works on God's plan and timetable, not mine. . . . God GOT ME! Amen!"

Akoy rehabbed through the spring of 2016. In late spring he met with former Central teammates at a pizza spot in midtown Omaha. Lotte showed up; she and Akoy were still a couple, though college and distance had tested them. The group included Tra-Deon Hollins and Tre'Shawn Thurman, both of whom played for UNO. Hollins had led the nation with 127 steals in 2015–16, an average of 3.96 per game. K. J. Scott, who started at guard for Texas Southern, was on hand, as was Dominique McKinzie. Even Eric

Behrens, who had left Central to coach at tiny Peru State College in 2014, dropped in to chat.

The mood was nostalgic, the conversation light and affectionate. Remember when Hollins was dehydrated and fainted at practice? How about when Akoy tripped as he ran the floor, or when he missed his dunk in the state final? Thurman's defensive lapses were a fertile source of ridicule. McKinzie was the king of trash talk. Scott's uncle was a pimp. "He came to a game and said something to Behrens at halftime," Hollins recalled. "Behrens got mad and said, 'I got a drunk pimp telling me my point guard needs to pass the ball.' And K. J. is like, 'Hey man, that's my uncle.' We were behind at half, and nobody could stop laughing. We were dying." Scott added, "I don't know why my mom brought him. He wanted to see his nephew, I guess. He had on a velvet sweatsuit."

Akoy shook with mirth. "Good memories," Behrens said. "For sure. The only glory days I got right now," Akoy said. Akoy's former coach did not reply, but his mind was plain to read: "It's early in the game, pal. Lots of time left on your clock."

Three and a half years past high school Akoy suited up for the Hoyas of Georgetown. He started a few games, then settled into a role as a reserve who rebounded and defended in the post and whose minutes fluctuated game to game. At his best Akoy's energy, effort, and fierce team ethos evoked NBA star Draymond Green. Georgetown played Creighton in Omaha before Akoy's family and friends and a hometown crowd of 17,626. Pumped with local vibes, he had 9 points, 9 rebounds, 3 blocks, and 5 turnovers in 22 minutes of a loss. "Akoy plays very hard," said coach John Thompson III. "You see that in his rebounds and effort. He was a little overzealous today being back home. We want him to bring that same intensity . . . but then stop trying to hit so many home runs on offense."

The trip was emotional because Lotte's mother, Ann Sjulin, had been diagnosed with breast cancer. Akoy took to Instagram and composed a message to Ann, accompanied by a selfie he had shot in a hospital bed:

This is a picture a little over a year ago as I was getting ready to go have my ACL surgery. As I sit here almost in tears, I cannot express how blessed by God I have been in my life. Through all my obstacles in life I have learned to become closer with God. While basketball is a big part of my life, I can say there is a lot more to life than that bouncing ball. As I think about my past 3 years of my career, I've also come to realize that my "problems" . . . are nothing compared to what others have gone and are going through. Shout out to my BestFriend, we will get through it together @babydocann!! With that, I say, I am blessed and all Glory to God. #GameDay #GloryToGod #WhyNotMe #Lights #Camera #Action #H4L.

"A lot more to life than that bouncing ball." With those words Akoy opened his future to the practical and pragmatic. He was twenty-two now, with mileage, scrapes, and dents. He posted a news report about an anti-fracking protest in Pennsylvania in which a youngish white man who opposed the protest taunted a black video journalist. The white man was filmed as he called the videographer a "lazy monkey" and "a chimp with a mop on his head." Akoy wrote: "Hmmmm. . . . America had changed. . . . America accepts everyone. . . . America is the best country in the world. . . . Questionable."

Soon came another post, about NFL quarterback Colin Kaepernick's refusal to stand for the national anthem in protest of racist policing: "God please help watch over the black people in this country. Along with those that are harmed regardless of race for no apparent reason at all. Amen!"

Then Akoy linked to a news report about a young African American girl in Charlotte, North Carolina. The girl, Zianna Oliphant, sobbed as she went before the city council and pleaded for a stop to police shootings of African Americans. "It's a shame that our fathers and mothers are killed and we can't see them anymore," Zianna said as tears streaked her face.

Akoy wrote: "A nine-year old having to make this plea is ridiculous!! Go ahead and make up an excuse America. (Yes it is not everyone in America is racist, I have been extremely blessed by the ones that aren't.) But for the ones that are, go ahead and just make up another excuse for everything. Now imagine if it was your white kid talking like this? Oh wait, you don't have to face issues like that, so you wouldn't know!!"

Akoy's tone caught the cultural zeitgeist. Donald Trump was elected president on an anti-immigration platform, which included a promise to build a Great Wall on the border with Mexico. He called for "an ideological certification to make sure that those we are admitting to our country share our values and love our people." Not a month into office he issued an executive order that suspended the entry to the United States of aliens from seven Muslim-majority countries: Iran, Iraq, Libya, Somalia, Syria, Yemen, and Sudan.

Five years after Arab Spring, Syria (5.5 million), Afghanistan (2.5 million), and South Sudan (1.4 million) led the world in refugee displacement. The *Central High Register* featured junior Elham Abdalla, a Muslim girl who had fled Sudan in 2014 with her father and two brothers. Elham's mother had died in Sudan, and she had become a surrogate mother for her brothers. She had been "very scared" when she came to Central as a freshman, but her ESL classes helped her adjust and fit in, and she had come to love Central and her teachers. Her biggest concern was the spike in paranoia about Muslims. "It makes me sad. . . . People blame all Muslim people for being terrorists," she said.

Central High now counted 6.7 percent of its students as ESL learners, up from 2.6 percent in Akoy's senior year. Refugee students comprised 5.4 percent, up from 2.3 percent, due to an influx from Bhutan and Nepal. Sixty-five different languages could be heard in the old wooden hallways. Federal data showed that Nebraska led the nation in resettling refugees per capita between October 2015 and September 2016. The state took in 1,441 refugees, or 76 per 100,000 Nebraskans. The United States as a whole took in 26 refugees per 100,000 residents.

A single case of tuberculosis reported at Omaha Benson High caused conservative Breitbart News to speculate if the student was one of 237 refugees at the school. School officials declined to say if the student was foreign-born or American-born, but Breitbart pointed out that many of

Omaha's refugee students came from countries "burdened by TB," such as Myanmar/Burma, Nepal, Somalia, and Bhutan. Foreign-born residents of Nebraska accounted for 82 percent of the thirty-eight cases of TB diagnosed in the state in 2014.

Refugee services were a work in progress. Ryan Overfield, who grew up near Omaha and whose wife was Kenyan, directed a Lutheran Family Services program to extend services to refugees beyond the initial ninety-day period, as well as to secondary migrants. "We're on track to serve four thousand people this year," Overfield said. "We help with food stamp applications, domestic violence, homelessness, and with children who have disabilities and need help navigating the system. If someone loses their job and faces eviction, I raise money so they don't lose their home. We also have two immigration attorneys, a full-time therapist, and interpretation services in twenty-six languages and dialects. Our goal is that refugees can walk into any service provider—health, courts, Head Start—and receive the same services."

Basketball had been Akoy's escape. Now it was not so much, as two of his mentors, Doluony and Hammer, pulled him in opposite directions. Doluony believed local high school and grassroots coaches had failed to prepare South Sudanese athletes—he and Akoy included—for elite college competition. He arranged for a South Sudanese prospect, Junub Char, to play at Blair Academy in New Jersey, where Luol Deng had played, and he sent another South Sudanese prospect, Ed Chang, to a shoe-sponsored grassroots team in Kansas City. Hammer, on the other hand, believed that the export of the best South Sudanese talent weakened his effort to attract grassroots shoe sponsorship, which in turn denied resources to the local base of South Sudanese players. Both Doluony and Hammer tugged on Akoy.

At Georgetown Akoy played with a torn meniscus and a swollen knee. A chronic strep throat added to his discomfort, as he averaged 15.4 minutes, 4.6 points, and 4.5 rebounds. Georgetown staggered through a 14-16 record for the season, at the end of which John Thompson III was fired. In the time it took Georgetown to hire NBA Hall of Famer and Hoya legend

Patrick Ewing as its new coach, Akoy had his knee repaired and his tonsils removed. Meanwhile, to complete his degree in liberal arts he needed to fulfill a foreign language requirement. Never bashful, Akoy went to the South Sudan embassy in Washington and made an unusual request. "I can speak Dinka, but I can't write it," he said. "Can you teach me to write Dinka?" Embassy staffers took to Akoy and taught him to write in his native language, and that satisfied Georgetown.

News from South Sudan was hellish. "People are starving," Akoy told me. "Organizations are trying to bring in food and water, and the government is not allowing it. They're on the brink of genocide. My grandma and dad's brother are still there. My grandma is moving back and forth to find a safe place. It's sad."

On May 20, 2017, Akoy received his diploma in front of his parents and siblings, a great-uncle, and the Hammers. "It was exciting; my parents were really proud," Akoy said. "I was the first in my family to graduate." The next day he returned to Omaha to prepare his future. A Georgetown degree was prestigious and could take him beyond the bouncing ball—just not yet, he decided, not while he retained two years of eligibility, not while he had fire in the belly. He would play as a graduate transfer at Southern Methodist University (SMU), in Dallas, and pursue a master's degree in business. He chose SMU over three other schools, he told an Omaha reporter, because it offered the best "showcase" for a player to make it as a pro. Though the NBA was a reach, pro leagues in Europe, Australia, Turkey, Russia, and China called out for talent, and SMU had a network of alumni on rosters in Europe. Akoy was encouraged when his high school teammate Hollins was drafted by the Fort Wayne Mad Ants of the NBA development league.

Behrens returned to Central after a three-year hiatus; he would coach his son Roman, a senior, just as his father had coached him twenty-five years ago. Lotte took the dental entrance exam and applied to dental schools. Time moved on. It would move beyond the bouncing ball, just not yet.

Akoy's decision brought to mind a quiet vignette. In late August 2016 I had arrived at his house with pen, pad, and voice recorder. Akoy was seated on his front porch, in T-shirt and shorts. Achan, his toddler sister, came out the door with a small rubber ball in her hands. She handed it to him and backed up. He bounced her the ball and she missed. He picked it up and prepared to bounce it again. "It's okay if you miss," he said. "Just gotta keep at it."

On November 23, 2017, Akoy took the floor for the Mustangs of SMU against Arizona. He became the first ever to play basketball for SMU after playing for Georgetown after playing for Louisville. Akoy averaged 5 points and 3.6 rebounds in 27 games but then soon was on the road again: in June 2018 he announced his return to Louisville for his final season of eligibility. From Sudan his nomad's journey had wound through Egypt, Maryland, Nebraska, and three universities, destination unknown, to be continued.

Postscript

POP

My grandfather, Benjamin Marantz, was a Russian Jewish immigrant who came to the United States in 1907 at the age of seventeen. He and two older brothers ran a small clothing store east of Pittsburgh, in Braddock, Pennsylvania, before he opened a store further west, in Weirton, West Virginia, in 1914. There was a new steel mill, and my grandfather sold work apparel to steelworkers, conversed with them in five languages, and over time expanded into Marantz's Department Store. He married, raised two children, and retired with my grandmother Mabel to Miami Beach in the late 1940s. "Pop," our term of endearment for him, was a soft-spoken and gentle man who died in 1961, before I knew to ask him about his youth.

Twenty years later I learned something of it from his younger sister, Fannie Block, who was in her mid-eighties and the only one of seven siblings still alive. Aunt Fannie told me her family lived in Bialystok, a city that was then in the Russian province of Belarus and now is in Poland. They worked in textiles and lived on the second floor of a three-story building. Bialystok had a large Jewish population, and like most eastern European cities of that era, plenty of gentiles who disliked Jews because they were supposed to.

One night when she was a little girl, Fannie recalled, a loud and angry mob armed with clubs and pickaxes came to their apartment building. They shouted from the street, up to the second floor windows: "Come out. Come out now. Or we will come in to get you." Her parents and older siblings barricaded and braced for the mob as it surged toward the front door of the building. Then the door opened, and the mob stopped dead in its tracks. In the entrance stood a uniformed officer of the Russian military with a loaded rifle. "Beat it, pea brains," he said—or the equivalent in the local dialect. "Move your dumb sorry asses away from here." The mob wasn't so dumb as to ignore a loaded gun, and it melted into the night. It had not known that the Russian officer who lived on the first floor was friendly with the Jewish family on the second floor.

That night the Marantz family decided to leave Russia. They thought of themselves as immigrants and were referred to as such, but they were refugees in the truest sense. What they fled was the Bialystok pogrom, which took place for three days in June 1906; in it at least eighty-one people were killed and another eighty wounded. One man described the violence: "Savages with axes and iron stakes have flung themselves, like the fiercest beasts, against the quiet villagers, whose sole crime was that they spoke another language and practiced another religion. . . . For this reason they smashed the skulls and poked out the eyes of men and women, of feeble old men and helpless infants!"

Those were the words of Ludovik Lazarus Zamenhof, who, like my grandfather, was Jewish and grew up in Bialystok. They were delivered at the second international conference of Esperanto, held in Geneva in 1906. Zamenhof spoke at the conference because he had created Esperanto, a new language he hoped could bring about nothing less than world peace, or as he wrote, "the unity of mankind."

Esperanto grew out of Zamenhof's experience with anti-Semitism. A deadly wave of pogroms had swept through Russia in 1881, when Zamenhof was in his early twenties, in Bialystok. Those pogroms gave rise to Zionism, by which the Jews would return to their promised land, Palestine, and escape the next pogrom that was sure to come. Zamenhof, an eye doctor by trade, embraced Zionism for a while until he became disillusioned with it. "Every nationalism presents for humanity only the greatest unhappiness," he wrote.

Zamenhof believed the source of international and interethnic conflict was language, with its Old Testament antecedent in Babel. A common language, he believed, would enhance empathy and brotherhood. In 1887 he self-published his first book on Esperanto, a primer, with explanations in Russian, and in 1888 he came out with his second book. His new language had an alphabet of twenty-eight letters, with most of the words derived from the Romance languages, and sixteen rules of grammar. Within two years his book was republished in German, Hebrew, Yiddish, Swedish, Latvian, Danish, Bulgarian, Italian, Spanish, French, Czech, and English. In 1905 the first international conference of Esperanto was held in France.

It was then that Zamenhof's vision of Esperanto as an agent for brotherhood met reality. Many viewed Esperanto only as a linguistic novelty and wanted no part of Zamenhof's moral crusade. The fact that Zamenhof was Jewish at a time of virulent anti-Semitism did not help his case. The conference committee asked him to delete from his keynote address a prayer to the spirit of brotherhood that, in the name of Esperantism, would unite humankind. The committee also issued a declaration that moral commitments had no bearing on Esperanto.

Zamenhof's description of the Bialystok pogrom at the second conference in 1906 was his effort to sustain his vision of Esperanto. "Break down, break down, the walls between the peoples," he said. "Give them the possibility of meeting and communication on a neutral basis, and only then those atrocities which we now see in various places will come to an end." When my grandfather fled Bialystok in 1907, he was a refugee of the hatred Zamenhof hoped to dispel. Zamenhof still clung to his idealistic vision when he died in 1917.

Esperanto spread through Europe and to Argentina, Algeria, Australia, and French Indochina, and an effort was made to establish it as the official language of the proceedings of the League of Nations. Esperanto was taught as a first language to children, among them the son of a Hungarian Jewish attorney who founded an Esperantist literary journal in Budapest. George Soros was born in 1930 and lived through the Nazi occupation of 1944–45 in which more than five hundred thousand Hungarian Jews were murdered and in which his family secured false identity papers to survive. When he and his father left Hungary in 1947, their first stop was at an Esperanto convention in Bern, Switzerland, and later that year Soros made speeches about world peace from the Esperanto speakers' stand in London's Hyde Park.

Soros studied at the London School of Economics, came to America in 1956, and amassed a multi-billion-dollar fortune in finance. Esperanto never became the global movement Zamenhof envisioned; indeed the spread of English rendered it a quaint hobby for a million or so practitioners. But Soros kept alive the initial spirit of Esperanto with his philanthropic Open Society Foundations. Out of the foundations came the International Migration Initiative to support refugees, migrants, and asylum seekers. The initiative supports legal action "aimed at ensuring governments meet their obligations under international law to treat all migrants with dignity, and offer them asylum when circumstances dictate."

Soros turned his attention to Sudan and South Sudan in 2012. After South Sudan had separated from Sudan, an estimated five hundred thousand people of South Sudanese origin who resided in Sudan were stripped of Sudanese citizenship. They had no legal status in Sudan and were exposed to arrest and detention and the threat of expulsion to South Sudan, their children were refused entry to schools and denied treatment at medical clinics, and they faced loss of livelihood and rights to their property. Affected groups included people with one parent from Sudan and one from South Sudan, people of complex mixed ancestry, and members of cross-border ethnic groups, among others. The affected groups were not guaranteed citizenship in South Sudan unless they could prove a link to the new country.

A Soros-funded group, the Open Society Initiative for Eastern Africa, published a series of recommendations: Sudan should not revoke citizenship unless an individual could acquire citizenship in South Sudan; citizenship should not be discriminatory and should be based on the norms set down in the African Charter on Human and Peoples' Rights; individuals had the right to due process regarding nationality status; the right to dual citizenship should be respected; and children's rights needed to be protected.

Neither side had the "political will" to implement the recommendations, according to their author, Bronwen Manby. But at the very least they had a blueprint in the event of democratic traction. A little more than one hundred years earlier, when my grandfather was made a refugee in Russia, there was no Open Society Initiative or George Soros to define his rights, only a fair-minded officer with a rifle. The Russian pogroms that drove him out also fueled Ludovik Zamenhof's creation of Esperanto and his vision of world brotherhood. In Soros, whose first language was Esperanto, intolerance found its logical extension and nemesis. Standing with Soros, and behind the UNHCR, is a growing movement to speak up for refugees, migrants, and asylum seekers. Which, I'm sure Pop would agree, is a start.

If my grandfather and Zamenhof were alive today, they might look around and conclude that the closest thing to a common language is sport. When nations convene at the Olympics, or World Cup for soccer, or World Baseball Classic, they get along in the language of sweat and competition, which is, in principle, democratic. Refugees and naturalized citizens gravitate to sport so that they can be seen and heard and valued in their adopted homelands. Sport invites them into the conversation. Some become fluent, and select others, such as Akoy Agau, become eloquent.

Notes

Because South Sudan became an autonomous region in 2005 and achieved formal independence in July 2011, pre-autonomy references are lowercase "south," while post-autonomy references are uppercase "South." Pre-autonomy references may be capitalized for rules of punctuation.

INTRODUCTION

xv   twenty million refugees: UNHCR, 2001 Statistical Yearbook, http://www .unhcr.org/3dcb7f666.html.

xv   "great survivors of our time": Kofi Annan, UN Press Release, June 18, 2001, http://www.un.org/press/en/2001/sgsm7848.doc.htm.

xvi   "a worldwide tragedy": Colin Powell, U.S. Department of State archives, https:// 2001-2009.state.gov/secretary/former/powell/remarks/2001/3694.htm.

xvi   "eyes of a heroine": Colin Powell, U.S. Department of State archives, https:// 2001-2009.state.gov/secretary/former/powell/remarks/2002/11310.htm.

xvii   forty-four million: UNHCR, 2011 Statistical Yearbook, http://www.unhcr .org/en-us/statistics/country/516282cf5/unhcr-statistical-yearbook-2011-11th -edition.html.

xvii   68.5 million: UNHCR, "Forced Displacement at Record 68.5 Million," http:// www.unhcr.org/en-us/news/stories/2018/6/5b222c494/forced-displacement -record-685-million.html.

1. ADAW

All quotations from Adaw Makier in this chapter are taken from author interviews.

1   unity and dignity: Francis Mading Deng, *The Dinka of Sudan* (Long Grove IL: Waveland Press, 1984).

1   division and conflict: Machar Wek Aleu-Baak, "Perceptions and Voices of South Sudanese about the North-South Sudan Conflict," Portland State University Library, January 2011, https://pdxscholar.library.pdx.edu/open _access_etds/184/.

1 imposed Arab customs: Dalal Mohamed Daoud, "Factors of Secession: The Case of South Sudan" (master's thesis, University of Saskatchewan, 2012).

5 peril of Sudanese non-Muslims: Country Reports on Human Rights Practices, U.S. Department of State, Bureau of Democracy, Human Rights, and Labor, 1999, https://www.state.gov/j/drl/rls/hrrpt/1999/273.htm.

8 refugee admissions dropped: Homeland Security, Office of Immigration Statistics, https://www.dhs.gov/xlibrary/assets/statistics/yearbook/2002/Yearbook2002.pdf.

2. FIRST THANKSGIVING

All quotations from Adaw Makier in this chapter are taken from author interviews.

10 refugee resettlement offices in twenty-one states: Church World Service history and background, https://cwsglobal.org/.

11 rented a house from a member: Liz F. Kay, "A Refugee Couple Finds Much to Be Thankful For," *Baltimore Sun*, November 28, 2002, http://articles.baltimoresun.com/2002-11-28/news/0211280289_1_southern-sudan-refugee-first-thanksgiving.

12 heard Manute Bol speak: "McDaniel Announces Diversity Week Events," *Baltimore Sun*, April 13, 2003.

12 "If I were in Sudan right now": Quoted in Leigh Montville, *Manute* (New York: Simon and Schuster, 1993), p. 214.

13 invited by the Sudanese government: Matt Schudel, "Manute Bol, a Former Washington Bullet and One of the NBA's Tallest Players, Dies at 47," *Washington Post*, June 20, 2010.

13 "led the way": Nicholas Kristof, "Most Valuable Helper," *New York Times*, June 23, 2010.

15 "the harsh reality of displacement": Ruud Lubbers, UNHCR press release, June 20, 2003, http://www.unhcr.org/en-us/admin/hcspeeches/3eeddda94/message-mr-ruud-lubbers-united-nations-high-commissioner-refugees-world.html.

3. STREET OF DREAMS

In this chapter author interviews are with, and quotations from, Mabel Boyd, Raydelle Meehan, Adaw Makier, Gutluak Kang, Tarir Gatuoch, and Akoy Agau.

16 elementary school from 1888 to 1983: Dick Ulmer, "Mason Past like Page of History," *Omaha World-Herald*, February 25, 1983.

17 South Sudanese arrived in Omaha: Refugee Empowerment Center history, http://refugeeempowerment.org/.

19 "we pledge to support": Colin Powell and Angelina Jolie, UNHCR press release, June 18, 2004, http://www.unhcr.org/en-us/news/latest/2004/6/40d2eb694/jolie-powell-launch-world-refugee-day-celebrations-washington-dc.html.

19 "Accept yourself as you are": John Ferak, "Sudanese People Gather in Honor of World Refugee Day," *Omaha World-Herald*, June 21, 2004.

21 "never give up hope": Antonio Guterres, UNHCR press release, June 20, 2006, http://www.unhcr.org/en-us/admin/hcspeeches/448e87d52/statement-mr-antonio-guterres-united-nations-high-commissioner-refugees.html.

4. PROPHECY

Unless otherwise noted, in this chapter author interviews are with, and quotations from, Akoy Agau, Tarir Gatuoch, Eric Behrens, Scott Hammer, Bruce Chubick, Dianne Chubick, Tim Cannon, Herb Welling, and Edward Bennett.

25 "change someone's life": Luol Deng, UNHCR public service announcement, World Refugee Day, 2008, https://www.youtube.com/watch?v=8klykfaMviU.

27 Texas booted a football player: "The Wild Wild Web: Social Networking Sites Offer Excitement, Traps for College Athletes," *Anderson Independent-Mail*, July 12, 2009.

27 social network rules: Pete Iorizzo, "Siena Players Go on Defense over Facebook," *Times Union* (Albany NY), October 21, 2009.

27 "be careful about what you post": "Obama's Q&A with 9th-graders," *Los Angeles Times*, September 8, 2009, http://latimesblogs.latimes.com/washington/2009/09/obama-chat-with-ninth-graders.html.

5. CENTRAL

Unless otherwise noted, in this chapter author interviews are with, and quotations from, A'Jamal Byndon, Linda Ganzel, Changkuoth Gatkuoth (formerly Lol Kuek), Rick Behrens, Gaylord "Doc" Moller, Eric Behrens, Herb Welling, Scott Hammer, Chad Burns, Jay Landstrom, Rod Mullen, Tim Shipman, and Akoy Agau.

32 first and oldest high school: Barry Combs and Jim Wigton, "Central High School Historical Timeline 1854–2016," Central High Foundation, http://www.chsfomaha.org/images/Documents/Historical-Timeline-Optimized.pdf.

32 later ran the *Omaha Bee*: David Bristow, *A Dirty Wicked Town: Tales of 19th Century Omaha* (Caldwell ID: Caxton Press, 2000).

33 Five generations of: Central High Foundation and "Historical Timeline."

33 Latino enrollment began to rise: Omaha Public Schools records.

33 Sudanese refugees arrived: *Omaha Central High O-Books*, 1998–2005.

40 "Create the Legacy": *Omaha Central High O-Book*, 2010, p. 13, http://omahachsarchives.org/yearbook.php.

6. TRUST

Unless otherwise noted, in this chapter author interviews are with, and quotations from, Akoy Agau, Eric Behrens, Jay Landstrom, Dominique McKinzie, and Rod Mullen.

46 he flipped a soft pass: YouTube, "Akoy Agau highlights," published July 9, 2010, by africanballer9. 1:06 to 1:10; https://www.youtube.com/watch?v=4ra3kTwxqOk&t=41s.

7. STARDOM

Unless otherwise noted, in this chapter author interviews are with, and quotations from, Eric Behrens, Jen Stastny, Adaw Makier, Scott Hammer, and Denise Powers.

47 "mature beyond his years": Ryly Jane Hambleton, "State Champs Have Underclassmen Filling Key Roles," *Lincoln Journal Star*, March 15, 2010.

47 "take me to college": Daria Seaton, *Central High Register*, February 4, 2010.

49 "refugees are survivors": Barack Obama, Proclamation 8538, World Refugee Day, June 18, 2010, http://www.presidency.ucsb.edu/ws/?pid=88069.

50 two-thirds of Americans opposed: Drew Desilver, "U.S. Public Seldom Has Welcomed Refugees into Country," Pew Research Center, November 19, 2015.

50 Franklin Roosevelt appeased: Richard Cohen, "FDR's Moral Failure on the Holocaust," *Washington Post*, March 11, 2013.

51 "last flickering light of humanity": Senator Pat McCarron, *Congressional Record*, March 2, 1953.

51 Displaced Persons Act of 1948: Harry Truman, "Special Message to the Congress on Aid for Refugees and Displaced Persons," Public Papers, March 24, 1952, https://www.trumanlibrary.org/publicpapers/index.php?pid=947.

51 refugees from Indochina: Edward Walsh, "U.S. Doubles Quota of Asian Refugees," *Washington Post*, June 29, 1979.

52 20,000 fewer: Refugee Council USA, http://www.rcusa.org/.

52 80,000 were too many: Refugee Resettlement Watch, https://refugee resettlementwatch.wordpress.com/.

52 celebrated the diversity: Mary Pipher, *The Middle of Everywhere* (Orlando FL: Harcourt, 2002).

53 "three Muslim brothers": Tom Andres, "The Muddle of Everywhere," Amazon customer review, April 25, 2004, https://www.amazon.com/gp/customer -reviews/R2JUJG1WEZWDTN/ref=cm_cr_arp_d_rvw_ttl?ie=UTF8&ASIN =0156027372.

54 upsurge in South Sudanese gangs: Kathleen Massara, "The Gangs of Omaha: Sudanese Who Fled Their War-Torn Country Face Growing Violence in Their Ranks," Alternet, December 7, 2010.

54 youngest player ever: "Basketball: Jays Back in Omaha League," *Omaha World-Herald*, June 28, 2010.

54 video of his highlights: You Tube, Akoy Agau highlights July 9, 2010, 3:12, published by africanballer9, https://www.youtube.com/watch?v= 4ra3kTwxqOk&t=38s. Video is no longer available.

8. TO ABSENT MOMS

Unless otherwise noted, in this chapter author interviews are with, and quotations from, Eric Behrens, Jay Ball, Akoy Agau, Paulino Gomez, and Edward Vinson.

58 "basically the whole United States": Nick Rubek, "Hoops Star Tackles Football," *Omaha World-Herald*, September 20, 2010.

59 taken out an insurance policy: David Lee Morgan Jr., *LeBron James: The Rise of a Star* (Cleveland: Gray and Company, 2003).

63 locker room talk: Jay Landstrom highlight video, 2010–11 season.

9. "TRUE FAITH AND ALLEGIANCE"

Unless otherwise noted, in this chapter author interviews are with, and quotations from, Charlotte "Lotte" Sjulin, Ann Sjulin, Dave Sjulin, Akoy Agau, Mike Sautter, Adaw Makier, Scott Hammer, Susan Mayberger, Keith Bigsby, and Michelle Synowiecki.

65 "to prepare young people": http://concordiaomaha.org/ (school website).

70 served about 1,350 refugee students: Omaha Public Schools ESL-Refugee Report 2011, http://district.ops.org/departments/GeneralFinanceand AdministrativeServices/Research/StatisticalReports/tabid/2338/Agg7692 _SelectTab/4/Default.aspx.

70 teen literacy centers: Erin Grace, "Young Refugees Race to Build Future," *Omaha World-Herald*, July 22, 2012.

72 "No one wants to become a refugee": Ban Ki-moon, "Secretary General's Message for 2011," UN.org, http://www.un.org/en/events/refugeeday/2011 /sgmessage.shtml.

72 Legislation proposed: "Leahy Introduces Refugee Protection Act," Senator Patrick Leahy press release, June 15, 2011, https://www.leahy.senate.gov/press /in-advance-of-world-refugee-day-leahy-introduces-refugee-protection-act.

73 Results were announced: "Sudanese Set Great Example," *Omaha World-Herald*, January 21, 2011.

73 Economic development was hamstrung: Ted Dagne, "The Republic of South Sudan: Opportunities and Challenges for Africa's Newest Country," Congressional Research Service, July 25, 2011.

74 PLAS: Nebraska Department of Education website, Persistently Lowest Achieving Schools, https://www.education.ne.gov/arra/plas.html.

10. @ZEROTHEHEROAKOY

Unless otherwise noted, in this chapter author interviews are with, and quotations from, Akoy Agau.

76 After its debut: "18 Million Twitter Users by End of 2009," Mashable, http:// mashable.com/2009/09/14/twitter-2009-stats/#wlxirzwocsqs.

76 4.2 million followers: Lahle Wolf, "Twitter Statistics," *The Balance*, September 23, 2016, https://www.thebalance.com/twitter-statistics-2008-2009-2010 -2011-3515899.

77 "it will stay there forever": Shaleigh Karnik, "Social Networking: Gift or Curse?" *Central High Register*, April 21, 2011.

77 dustbin for anonymous snark: "#Central Probs Twitter Account Paints a Negative Picture of Central," editorial, *Central High Register*, January 6, 2012.

11. FAMILIES

Unless otherwise noted, in this chapter author interviews are with, and quotations from, Akoy Agau, Amadu Swaray, Ann Sjulin, Dave Sjulin, Lotte Sjulin, Bette Ball, and Paul Nielson.

86 Marital stress: Amadu Swaray, "Divorce Rate amongst African Immigrants," Swaray Law Office LTD, August 24, 2010, http://www.swaraylawoffice.com /2010/08/divorce-rate-amongst-african-immigrants/.

12. PERFECTION

In this chapter author interviews are with, and quotations from, Doug Goltz, Eric Behrens, and Tre'Shawn Thurman.

92   could make Nebraska history: Nebraska State Activities Association, basketball history/records, https://nsaahome.org/basketball/.

93   "run the table": "Expectations High for Eagles," *Omaha World-Herald*, December 1, 2011.

95   "learned to block softly": Ryly Jane Hambleton, "Agau Comfortable Holding Court on the Court," *Lincoln Journal Star*, March 24, 2013.

95   "controlled chaos": Sam McKewon, "Central's Dynasty," *Omaha World-Herald*, March 7, 2012.

95   "kind of got lazy": Nick Rubek, "Agau Helps No. 1 Central Pull Away," *Omaha World-Herald*, January 28, 2012.

96   "really bothering him": Stu Pospisil, "Agau Has Surgery, May Play in Districts," *Omaha World-Herald*, February 20, 2012.

96   "Some of the words": Sam McKewon, "Central's Dynasty," *Omaha World-Herald*, March 7, 2012.

98   "pressure situation": Ken Hambleton, "Omaha Central Squeaks Past Bears," *Lincoln Journal Star*, March 9, 2012.

99   Behrens congratulated his players: Jay Landstrom highlight video, 2011–12 season.

13. BASKETBALL AND BUSINESS

Unless otherwise noted, in this chapter author interviews are with, and quotations from, Ann Sjulin, Adaw Makier, Denise Powers, Keith Bigsby, Scott Hammer, and Leisha Hammer.

103   It capped attendance: Jonathon Braden, "Central Turns Away 200 or So Hopefuls—the Downtown High School Is out of Room and Joins Burke in Capping Enrollment," *Omaha World-Herald*, March 5, 2012.

103   Bigsby, who told a reporter: Braden, "Central Turns Away 200 or So Hopefuls," *Omaha World-Herald*, March 5, 2012.

104   described a player: ESPN Scouting Report, http://insider.espn.com/college-sports/basketball/recruiting/player/evaluation/_/id/102637/akoy-agau.

106   Within four years: Kurt Badenhausen, "LeBron James Tops the NBA's Highest-Paid Players 2016," *Forbes*, January 20, 2016, https://www.forbes.com/sites/kurtbadenhausen/2016/01/20/lebron-james-tops-the-nbas-highest-paid-players-2016/#c389ed64508e.

106 NBA minimum salary: "NBA Annual Salary Scale," http://www.nba.com/news /cba_minimumsalary_050804.html.

106 $99 average ticket price: statista.com, https://www.statista.com/statistics /220764/nba-average-ticket-price-for-los-angeles-lakers-games/.

107 Pitino would make: "Pitino, Calipari among Highest-Paid College Basketball Coaches", USA Today, July 1, 2013.

107 The average pay: https://www.aaup.org/reports-publications/2013 -14salarysurvey.

107 Kentucky woman was convicted: Shaun Assael, "Rick Pitino Extortion Trial: The Full Story," espn.com, September 20, 2010.

108 In February 2018 the NCAA would vacate: Jeff Greer, "Louisville Forced to Vacate 2013 Men's Basketball Title after NCAA Denies Appeal," USA Today, February 20, 2018, https://www.usatoday.com/story/sports/ncaab/2018/02 /20/louisville-forced-vacate-2013-mens-basketball-title-after-ncaa-denies -appeal/355189002/.

14. TEMPTATION AND DECISION

Unless otherwise noted, in this chapter author interviews are with, and quotations from, Akoy Agau, Eric Behrens, Tre'Shawn Thurman, Keith Bigsby, Tra-Deon Hollins, Dave Sjulin, Scott Hammer, and Leisha Hammer.

116 allegations surfaced: Katina Powell, Breaking Cardinal Rules (Indianapolis: IBJ Book Publishing, 2015).

117 infamous rant about Boston: Matt Dolloff, "Negativity Sucks: 5 Famous Sports Figures Who Infamously Blamed the Media for Their Problems," CBS Boston, November 13, 2015, http://boston.cbslocal.com/2015/11/13/5-sports-figures -blame-media-problems/.

15. STANDING BEAR AND BRANDO

In this chapter author interviews are with, and quotations from, Michele Roberts, Akoy Agau, Jen Stastny, and Jay Ball.

119 Holocaust Literature: Gerda Weissman Klein, All but My Life (New York: Hill and Wang, 1957).

120 The Ponca were a peaceful tribe: Joe Starita, I Am a Man (New York: St. Martin's Griffin, 2008).

121 "a citizen beyond all dispute": Starita, I Am a Man, pp. 144, 145, 150, 151, 157.

123 hired as a secretary: Susan Mizruchi, Brando's Smile (New York: Norton, 2014).

123 Dodie Brando was a mainstay: Omaha Community Playhouse website, http:// www.omahaplayhouse.com/about/view/history/.

124 Fonda played opposite: Bob Fischbach, "As the Omaha Community Playhouse Turns 90, We Look Back at Its Rich History," *Omaha World-Herald*, March 30, 2015.

124 allegory and critique: Karina Longworth, "On the Waterfront, Elia Kazan (Blacklist Episode #13)," May 23, 2016, in *You Must Remember This*, podcast, 47:45, http://www.youmustrememberthispodcast.com/episodes/2016/5/23/on-the-waterfront-elia-kazan-blacklist-episode-13.

125 as Brando wrote in his autobiography: Robert Lindsey, *Brando: Songs My Mother Taught Me* (New York: Random House, 1994).

125 Along the way he met: Andrew Morton, *Angelina: An Unauthorized Biography* (New York: St. Martin's, 2010).

125 philanthropic nonprofit: Guidestar.org.

126 promoted Jolie: UNHCR.org, "Special Envoy Angelina Jolie," http://www.unhcr.org/en-us/special-envoy-angelina-jolie.html.

126 "I honestly believe": Angelina Jolie, *Notes from My Travels* (New York: Pocket Books, 2003).

16. DYNASTY BLUES

In this chapter author interviews are with, and quotations from, Eric Behrens, Herb Welling, Rod Mullen, Jen Rooney, and Emily Beck.

127 Milan High had an enrollment: "The Milan Miracle of 1954," milan54.org, http://milan54.org/milan-miracle-1954/.

128 Akoy the highest-rated: Rivals.com, rivals 150, 2013 Prospect Ranking, https://n.rivals.com/prospect_rankings/rivals150/2013.

129 Huntington Prep: https://www.huntingtonprep.com/huntingtonprepprogram (Huntington Prep website).

130 ranked it twentieth: Maxpreps.com, High School Basketball Rankings, 2012, http://www.maxpreps.com/rankings/basketball-winter-11-12/1/national.htm.

132 "We had to prove": Stu Pospisil, "Eagles Know Tough Game Still Ahead," *Omaha World-Herald*, December 20, 2012.

132 "They're in tears": Stu Pospisil, "California Power's Late 3 Sinks Central," *Omaha World-Herald*, December 20, 2012.

132 "Nebraska has some jewels": Stu Pospisil, "After a Taste of Respect, Eagles Hungry for More," *Omaha World-Herald*, December 21, 2012.

17. FOUR!

In this chapter author interviews are with, and quotations from, Eric Behrens, Tre'Shawn Thurman, Jay Landstrom, Henry Hawbaker, Tim Shipman, Tra-Deon Hollins, and Akoy Agau.

134 Fifty-five D-1 scholarship players: Oak Hill Academy basketball website, http://www.oakhillhoops.com/home.

137 "a signature win": Stu Pospisil, "Huge Feather in Nest: Omaha Central's Eagles Scored Arguably the Most Prestigious Win in State Prep History, but Still Want More," *Omaha World-Herald*, February 11, 2013.

139 "Harlem Globetrotters": Dirk Chatelain, "Turning Class A into Washington Generals," *Omaha World-Herald*, March 10, 2013.

18. SPRING PROM

Unless otherwise noted, in this chapter author interviews are with, and quotations from, Ann Sjulin, Akoy Agau, Henry Hawbaker, Thor Tripp, Denise Powers, Jacob Bigelow, and Edward Bennett.

141 Eagles Basketball Day: Joe Duggan, "Gov. Heineman Honors Central High Basketball Team with Official Day," *Omaha World-Herald*, March 18, 2013.

141 "Harlem Shake": "All-State Shake Video," Omaha.com, March 23, 2013, https://www.youtube.com/watch?v=rxwlr6gsz5k.

142 "leaned over the balcony ledge": Ryly Jane Hambleton, "Agau Comfortable Holding Court on the Court," *Lincoln Journal Star*, March 24, 2013.

144 "same look on his face": Sam McKewon, "Omaha Central Star Agau Has Plenty to Smile about," *Omaha World-Herald*, March 7, 2013.

144 "things that Coach P has done": Akoy Agau, "Akoy Agau in His Words on Louisville Basketball in the Final Four," *Courier-Journal*, April 6, 2013.

19. REPATRIATION

In this chapter author interviews are with, and quotations from, Chang-kuoth Gatkuoth, Akoy Agau, Nancy Peter, Bernadita Peter, Mabel Boyd, and Raydelle Meehan.

146 When shooting began: Steve Liewer, "South Sudanese in Omaha Mourn Their Holiday Season," *Omaha World-Herald*, December 20, 2014.

146 Among the Nuer partisans: Steve Liewer, "UNO Grad Shuttles between Omaha, South Sudan Homeland for One Cause: Democracy," *Omaha World-Herald*, November 1, 2015.

147 "This event is about unity": Luol Deng, "South Sudan Unite: A Message from Luol Deng," You Tube, June 20, 2016, https://www.youtube.com/watch?v=sdz6etmgmiA&feature=share.

148 "murders of civilians": Adrian Edwards, "South Sudan Fighting Drives Surge of Refugees to Uganda," UNHCR, July 26, 2016, http://www.unhcr.org/afr

/news/latest/2016/7/57973cde4/south-sudan-fighting-drives-surge-refugees
-uganda.html.

148 "children as young as two years old": Doctors without Borders,
"Responding to Cholera Outbreak in Juba," July 29, 2016, http://www
.doctorswithoutborders.org/article/south-sudan-responding-cholera
-outbreak-juba.

20. GETTING IT RIGHT

In this chapter author interviews are with, and quotations from, Koang
Doluony.

151 organizer Manyang G. Berberi: South Sudanese Australian National
Basketball Association on Facebook, https://www.facebook.com/pg
/southsudaneseau/about/?ref=page_internal.

151 began to funnel its best players: Damien Cave, "South Sudanese, Seeking
to Fit In, Stand Out in Australian Basketball," *New York Times*, May 3, 2017.

151 up to thirty had played: "Players from South Sudan," realGM.com, https://
basketball.realgm.com/info/nationality/11/South-Sudan/M.

155 marriage of underage south Sudanese girls: Stephen Buttry, "An Unhappy
Marriage: Sudanese Custom, U.S. Law," *Omaha World-Herald*, March
11, 2001.

157 "some will be basketballers": Steve Liewer, "South Sudanese Leader Tells
Omaha: Young People Are Key to Future, and to Peace," *Omaha World-
Herald*, October 6, 2015.

21. BEYOND

Unless otherwise noted, in this chapter author interviews are with, and
quotations from, Akoy Agau, Eric Behrens, Tra-Deon Hollins, Tre'Shawn
Thurman, K. J. Scott, Dominique McKinzie, and Ryan Overfield.

159 suspended one game: Marjie Ducey, "Former Omaha Prep Star Agau Suspended at Louisville," *Omaha World-Herald*, December 20, 2013.

160 Georgetown played Creighton: Jon Nyatawa, "Georgetown's Akoy Agau
'Plays Very Very Hard' in Omaha Return," *Omaha World-Herald*, February
19, 2017.

162 "an ideological certification": Philip Bump, "Here's What Donald Trump
Said in His Big Immigration Speech," *Washington Post*, August 31, 2016,
https://www.washingtonpost.com/news/the-fix/wp/2016/08/31/heres-what
-donald-trump-said-in-his-big-immigration-speech-annotated/?utm_term
=.2a0a78744e8a.

162   led the world in refugee displacement: "Global Trends: Forced Displacement in 2016," UNHCR Statistics, http://www.unhcr.org/en-us/statistics/unhcrstats /5943e8a34/global-trends-forced-displacement-2016.html.

162   Muslim girl who had fled Sudan: Zoia Morrow, "Finding Home," *Central High Register*, October 12, 2016.

162   6.7 percent of its students: Omaha Public Schools statistics, ops.org.

162   Federal data showed: Emily Nohr, "A Welcoming State: Nebraska Led the Nation in Resettling Most Refugees per Capita in the Last Year," *Omaha World-Herald*, December 9, 2016.

162   tuberculosis reported: Michael Patrick Leahy, "Student Diagnosed with TB at Nebraska School Where 18 Percent Are Refugees," Breitbart.com, December 9, 2016.

22. POSTSCRIPT

In this chapter author interviews are with, and quotations from, Bronwen Manby.

168   "Savages with axes": Esther Schor, *Bridge of Words: Esperanto and the Dream of a Universal Language* (New York: Metropolitan Books, 2016). Quotes from Zamenhof in this chapter are from this work.

169   lived through the Nazi occupation: David Mikics, "The Secret Language of George Soros," Tabletmag.com, October 26, 2016.

170   International Migration Initiative: Migration Initiative quotes are from Open Society Foundations website: Migration & Asylum, https://www .opensocietyfoundations.org/topics/migration-asylum.

170   a series of recommendations: Bronwen Manby, "International Law and the Right to Nationality in Sudan," Open Society Justice Initiative, February 2011.

Index

National College Athletic Associa-
tion. *See* NCAA
nativism, 50, 53
Naturalization Oath, 48, 67
Nazi occupation, 169
NBA, 12, 23; Orlando Magic vs. Utah
Jazz, 101; player salaries, 106; Players
Association "Top 100" camp, 105
NCAA, 81, 104, 106; and recruiting
violations, 107–8
Nebraska, xv, xviii, 14–15, 20, 32, 40, 71,
73, 155; and Akoy Agua, 80, 90, 92–
93, 97, 99–100, 114; and basketball,
128, 133, 135–38; and Ponca, 120–21;
and refugee resettlement, 162–63
Nielson, Paul, 87
ninemillion.org, 21
Nuer tribe, 19, 53, 146–47

Obama, Barack, 27, 49–51, 67, 119
Obama, Michelle, 133
Oden, Greg, 97
Office of Refugee Resettlement, 17
Okafor, Jalil, 133
Omaha Central Eagles Basketball Day, 141
Omaha Community Playhouse, 123–24
Omaha middle school, 38
Omaha NE, 14; AAU in, 23–24, 26, 38,
54, 115; Baptist Church in, 18–19;
and basketball, 39, 44–46, 62–64,
93–99, 134–37; and Central High
School, xv, 32, 40, 121, 154–55, 162;
First Lutheran Church in, 19; his-
tory of, 16, 120–25; Mason School
Apartments in, 16–17; and meat-
packing industry, 16; and refugees,
14, 162; Sudanese Center in, 18

Omaha Public Library, 71
Omaha Public Schools, 17; and refu-
gee students, 70
Omaha Refugee Task Force, 17
Omaha Talons, xi, 151–52, 157
Omaha Workforce Development, 17
Omaha World Herald, 47, 93, 95, 137,
139–41
Omdurman, Sudan, 4
O'Neil, Shaquille, 76
On the Waterfront, 124
Open Door Mission, 154
Open Society Foundation, 170
Open Society Initiative for Eastern
Africa, 170.
Overfield, Ryan, 10, 163
Oxfam America, 12

Pakistan, 21, 125
Partee, Michael, 39
PASS (Positively Affecting Student
Success), 47
Pennebaker, Bess, 123
Peter, Bernadita, 148–49
Peter, Nancy, 148–49
Phillips, Terrence, 135
Pipher, Mary, 52–53
Pitino, Rick, 107–8; and Akoy Agau,
115–17, 131, 142, 144, 159; coaching
career of, 116–17
Ponca Tribe, 120–23
Poppleton, Andrew Jackson, 121–22
Pospisil, Stu, 137
Powell, Colin, xv, 19
Powell, Katina: *Breaking Cardinal
Rules: Basketball and the Escort
Queen*, 116